MOUNTAIN DREAMERS

Visionaries of Sierra Nevada Skiing

Robert Frohlich

Photographs by Carolyn Caddes and Tom Lippert

COLDSTREAM PRESS

Cover and book design: Andrea Hendrick

Editors: Laurel Hilde Lippert, S.E. Humphries

Production: Carroll Harrington

Photographic reproduction: Spindler Photographic Services, San Francisco

Printed in Hong Kong by Palace Press International, San Francisco

Coldstream Press

P.O. Box 9590

Truckee, CA 96162

916.587.4287   Fax 916.587.9081

E-mail wendin@sierra.net

Publisher's Cataloging in Publication Data

Frohlich, Robert.

    Mountain dreamers: visionaries of Sierra Nevada skiing/Robert
    Frohlich; photographs by Carolyn Caddes and Tom Lippert.
    p. cm
    Includes index.
    Preassigned LCCN: 97-66550
    ISBN: 0-9633056-5-4 (hbk)
    ISBN: 0-9633056-6-2 (pbk)

    1. Skiers—Sierra Nevada (Calif. and Nev.)—Biography. I.
    Caddes, Carolyn, 1935 –. II Lippert, Tom. III Title

    GV854.2.A1F76 1997   796.93'5'097944
                         QBI97-40494

    10 9 8 7 6 5 4 3 2 1

In recognition of our shared responsibility to preserve the environment, Palace Press International will plant two trees to replace every tree that was harvested to produce the paper to print this book.

Mountain Dreamers was written, designed and produced using Adobe PageMaker 6.5, Adobe Illustrator 6.02 and Adobe Photoshop 4.0 running on Macintosh Power PCs 6100/66 and 8500/180. Text was prepared in Microsoft Word 5.0. The photographs were scanned on an Epson ES-1000C and HP IIcx. The type was composed in Minion Multiple Master, Novarese and Xstacy Sans Medium.

Dedicated to the memory of Steve McKinney who pushed me and continues to push me towards excellence. A day does not pass that I do not think of his wonderful spirit, his sense of humor and his love for planet Earth.

"...mountains were meant to see over,
Stairs from the valleys and steps to
the sun's retreats."

Earle Birney

ACKNOWLEDGEMENTS

To create the gentle pull and soft release of words
an author needs a lot of help.

Publisher Ellie Huggins bypassed all the ways in which one gets a job. She looked past my awkwardness, my broken down car, my disorganized life and somehow saw that I was the writer she wanted for the project. I thought then and I think now, that to be seen in this way by another human being is the most precious of gifts.

Hashing out copy with editor Laurel Hilde Lippert, especially with my first efforts, was a lifelong learning experience. Laurel, in her quiet pensive manner, taught, guided and prodded. Her ability to distill and revise material added an authorship to the book.

It was a privilege to work with Carolyn Caddes. Her photography is only outdone by her humor and delightful outlook on life. Carolyn helped inspire copy through her images of our subjects.

Others helped inspire too. Dick Dorworth cooked pasta and talked the whole thing out one night in his cabin below the Grand Teton in Wyoming. His advice and encouragement were immeasurable. Kaitlin Klaussen put up with my complaints and self-doubt with a gentleness that only she possesses. Artist Liz McMillan provided me with inspiration at a pivotal time when segments of the book had to get done. Deacon Chapin constantly lent moral support, exclaiming time and again, "You can do it!" Bobbie and Topper Hagerman provided assistance and a place for Carolyn to crash when taking photos of Jimmie Heuga in Colorado.

Without a kick in the pants from journalist Tanya Branson, I never could have started this project. Then again, without my second grade classroom teacher, Mrs. Danner, I never would have learned to read. That lady tutored me at her house every Saturday morning in front of a glass of milk. It was my mother, Billie, who first taught me how to write. "Write like you're talking to the person in front of you," she still lectures. Maxwell Steele, my creative writing professor at North Carolina, helped mother's advice mature into a profession.

I am grateful to those who provided me with the information to write the material for this book. Jimmie Heuga, no matter how busy, always called back. Architect Henrik Bull stopped whatever he was drawing to answer persistent questions. Construction maverick Tom Dempsey allowed me into his office with very short notice. Marty Arrougé, Stu Campbell, John Fry, Frank Helm, Don Schwartz, Pat O'Donnell, Stan Walton and Jurgen Wetzstein all divulged vital information. Nancy McCoy at Heavenly was indispensable with research, and so was Wendy Kelly at Mammoth. Yosemite's Linda Eade responded efficiently to requests. Auburn Ski Club's Bill Clark provided me with school-high piles of information about numerous ski resorts. Liz Dugan made the Squaw Valley segment possible. Craig Beck lent information and photos. My sister, Margaret, gave both financial and moral support.

I am indebted, finally, to the ski pioneers of the Sierra Nevada who are the substance of this creation. Their cooperation, graciousness and friendship will never be forgotten. "Pursue your passion. Be true to your friends," Wayne Poulsen once told a young ski writer years ago. God bless you, sir.

Robert Frohlich, 1997

CONTENTS

FOREWORD

—

ANDREA MEAD

LAWRENCE

My Magnetic North:
The Sierra Nevada

*There is much comfort
in high hills
and a great easing
of the heart.*

Geoffrey Winthrop Young

ike a compass needle, my soul restlessly seeks its own magnetic north: the Sierra Nevada. In cities I feel closed in. Leaving them, I follow my compass home to the Sierra, where a great weight is lifted from my spirit by some indefinable power of Sierra light and space.

My personal magnetic north has always been in mountains. From the Green Mountains of Vermont to the Sierra Nevada, mountains link me to other people in a widespread web that touches many of the visionaries in this book:

Charley Proctor designed and built the first ski trail, Sunset Schuss, at Pico Peak, Vermont, the ski area my parents built in the mid-30s and where they are now buried on Sunset Schuss.

Cortlandt "Corty" Hill, an early Sierra Nevada skier and a friend of Dave McCoy, managed the first U.S. Olympic ski team I was on (1948). I named my first child for Corty Hill, and Corty Lawrence calls the Sierra home.

Nic Fiore guided me and a friend to Yosemite's Ostrander Lake when, shortly after arriving in California, I felt a deep need for mountains.

Jill Kinmont's life first touched mine at Alta in 1955. Mountains have defined both our lives; we share a love of the Eastern Sierra and both call it home.

Gus Weber's path and mine first crossed in Wyoming at my brother's 1959 wedding and again on my first Sierra backpack. He shared with my children the ease and confidence he possesses when in the mountains.

Dave McCoy dreamed and built Mammoth Mountain ski area above Mammoth Lakes, my home.

With many of these visionaries, I share profound physical and spiritual ties to mountains—ties forged by meeting the slopes and peaks on their own terms. Most of us first ascended mountains not in chairlifts but on foot. We pushed upward, fueled by food grown on plains that were once mountain slopes, watered by streams from mountain snowcaps. We were one with mountains; we *had* to share that challenging but transcendent experience!

Mountain skiing is now easier, more accessible and safer, but I believe that the very early difficulty of ascending the slopes helped create the hardiness and the vision of the people who are chronicled in this book. I doubt that we are creating such new pioneers in the soft, mechanized ski areas of today. Perhaps we will see them emerging from the cross-country and telemarking back country skiers who forge their own paths in the mountains.

Many of today's ski areas are owned by large corporations that have no real connection with the grandeur of the mountains and the adventurous spirit that motivated the ski area founders and skiers of yesteryear. Before we dishonor the very qualities that drew us all to the mountain, let us admit that our glorious mountains do not exist for our ends. For billions of people, mountains are sacred, and the Sierra visionaries feel this reverence in their very bones and heart.

© Carolyn Caddes

My parents gave me the gift of mountains at my birth, and ever since then, mountains have been the defining force in my life.

Above Lake Tahoe.

INTRODUCTION

ELLIE
HUGGINS
—
TRUCKEE
CALIFORNIA
MAY 1997

As a child I always knew that I was happier in the mountains than at the sea shore, and certainly in the countryside rather than the city. But the mountains of my childhood were the green-clad peaks of the Adirondacks and mountains of Vermont. Coming West for the first time as a young bride, I was introduced to the shining granite of the Sierra Nevada when camping at Glacier Point in Yosemite National Park. Later, I skied at Badger Pass and then at Sugar Bowl and the emerging resorts of Lake Tahoe. Every winter I would wait expectantly for that first storm so that I could return to the Sierra, and every summer I packed the kids in the car the day after school let out to go to Yosemite Valley to camp and explore. My dreams were always of winter fields of snow or of summer wildflowers. Finally, like the dreamers in this book, I moved to the mountains permanently, able to walk out my door for winter skiing or for a summer hike in the woods and pursue the publication of books about the Sierra Nevada by Coldstream Press.

For several years I had planned a book about the ski areas in the Sierra, but the project always stayed in the background because the subject seemed too big. However, when I heard the news of Wayne Poulsen's death, I realized that the collective memory of the men and women who created the sport of downhill skiing in the Sierra might vanish if someone did not reach them soon to record their personal memories of those early days.

At that moment, the idea for *Mountain Dreamers: Visionaries of Sierra Nevada Skiing* was born. I had known Carolyn Caddes and admired the exceptional photographs in her book *Portraits of Success: Impressions of Silicon Valley Pioneers*. I asked her to join the project. I had read Robert "Fro" Frohlich's fine tribute to Wayne Poulsen in *Sierra Heritage* magazine and contacted him about writing the book. Laurel Hilde Lippert had been editor for Coldstream's other books and, as a pilot, could fly her husband, photographer Tom Lippert, for the aerial photographs of the Sierra. Andrea Hendrick, an award-winning designer and personal friend, signed on to create a work of art from their combined efforts. With the support of old friends, computer and production guru Carroll Harrington and veteran newspaper editor S.E. Humphries, I had a team to make a dream into a book.

As Fro and I discussed the project we realized that we were not going to write the definitive history of Sierra Nevada skiing. We wanted the book to be about the people who were passionate about the sport of downhill skiing and developed the ski areas that brought people to the mountains in the winter. He introduced me to Bill Berry and his importance as the chronicler and active participant of skiing in the Sierra from its infancy on Hilltop at Truckee. Bill had skied with Wayne Poulsen to scout the location of Mount Rose Upski, ridden the West's first chairlift on Sugar Bowl's opening day in 1939, reported on the 1960 Winter Olympic Games, founded the William B. Berry Western America Skisport Museum at Boreal and created its first exhibits.

He discovered the 19th century longboard racers at La Porte, California, and wrote their story in his book, *Lost Sierra: Gold, Ghosts & Skis*. The choice to include Bill Berry was easy, but what about the other mountain dreamers?

From the shining granite of John Muir's Yosemite and Lake Tahoe's Desolation Wilderness to the castellated peaks near Donner Summit, the Sierra Nevada attracted mountain lovers to its towns. Many who came could not bear to leave, finding ways to stay and make a living. Among those who arrived were pioneer ski instructors, lured to the Lake Tahoe and Yosemite ski areas in the 1930s. Charley Proctor came to Yosemite Valley from the well-established ski traditions of Dartmouth Ski Club and stayed as director of winter sports for the park for almost forty years. Nic Fiore has directed the Badger Pass Ski School since 1958 and is still going strong. Young Austrians, like Hannes Schroll and Bill Klein, helped make Sugar Bowl into a ski area beloved by skiers, movie stars and society matrons from the Bay Area. Dave McCoy first fell in love with the Mammoth Lakes area on a trip there when he was twelve and returned to bring his joy of skiing to hundreds of thousands at Mammoth Mountain. Wayne Poulsen was introduced to Squaw Valley by Marty Arrougé, the son of a Basque sheepherder from Reno. He founded Squaw Valley Ski Corporation with Alex Cushing in 1948. Jo Marillac directed the Ski School at Squaw Valley and helped Cushing secure the 1960 Winter Olympic Games. The list also includes people with different dreams: owners of small ski areas like Donner Ski Ranch, Sierra Ski Ranch, Dodge Ridge and Bear Valley that continue to lure thousands of day skiers to their mountains every weekend. Peter Klaussen and Dick Reuter envisioned the trails for Alpine Meadows and Kirkwood, planned them and in Reuter's case, personally cut the trees, installed the water lines and managed the mountain. Nick Badami at Alpine Meadows and Bill Killebrew at Heavenly kept the dreams alive during the drought years with their special vision and talents. Finally, Bill Jensen's leadership at Northstar-at-Tahoe helped define how Sierra Nevada ski areas can meet the multiple challenges of the 1990s.

As the project progressed, we realized that the story was not complete without recognizing ski instructors who have had an impact on the sport. We decided to include a few—from the pioneer Luggi Foeger, who started at Badger Pass and directed the school at Alpine Meadows and later designed Ski Incline, to Stan Tomlinson who has been at Squaw Valley since 1955 and still teaches an occasional lesson. Werner Schuster was brought to Alpine Meadows by Luggi Foeger, followed him as director of the ski school and later became involved in marketing. Babette Haueisen, recognized by *SKI* magazine in 1995 as one of the top 100 ski instructors in the country, is teaching her fourth generation of skiers.

Fro interviewed Jill Kinmont Boothe as part of Dave McCoy's story to learn more about the winning Mammoth Race Program. We decided to include Jill and two other inspirational racers who have overcome obstacles in their lives with uncommon courage. I was privileged to come to know Jimmie Heuga and Tamara McKinney through their poignant stories.

Perhaps the most exciting part of the project for me was to meet most of the dreamers during the sessions with photographer Carolyn Caddes. The natural setting that we chose and Carolyn's consummate skill allowed me to get to know these remarkable people. I enjoyed hearing their stories as she set up her camera and lights. I watched as Carolyn cajoled and laughed with them and captured the spirit of these men and women on film.

However, it was not until I learned of Chris Kuraisa's unexpected death just a few months after we photographed him and of the devastation of Alex Cushing's house and piano in the January 1997 flood and of Bill Jensen's sudden departure from Northstar three days after he smiled into Carolyn's camera that I knew that the book was meant to be. We were blessed to have a team that could make my own dream a reality in less than a year.

The mountain dreamers whose memories fill this book are the extraordinary men and women who fell in love with the Sierra Nevada, built the ski areas in the snowy range and taught legions of first-time skiers as well as numerous men and women who are among the world's leading ski racers. Many of their dreams have turned to gold and we are all the richer for their devotion to the sport called downhill skiing.

© Carolyn Caddes

Nic Fiore and publisher Ellie Huggins review the photographs for the book. Upon seeing the photo of Andrea Mead Lawrence, Nic immediately remembered skiing with her to Ostrander hut.

*"Schniebs was right you know.
It was Otto Schniebs who said,
'Skiing is a way of life.'
Boy, was he right.
I'll never forget that.
Skiing sure has changed
and for the better.
We had a lot more broken legs,
but, what the hell,
a broken leg doesn't matter
when you love the sport."*

illiam B. Berry, historian emeritus of the U.S. Ski Association sweeps through ski tales in a rapid-fire show and tell. "Skiing is the world's idolized sport. It's like being bitten by a virus." His words are like the sport itself—energetic, colorful and expansive.

Although he pads stiffly around his Reno home with a cane for support, Bill Berry's memory is extremely sharp and clear for a man nearing the century mark. In a moment, he's back at Hilltop in Truckee, California, about to ride the Sierra's first uphill tow on a clear December day, almost seventy years ago. "I rented a pair of skis made from pine that had a single strap over the boot. Beyond the lodge stood an amazing contraption called a 'pullback.' A tow ride cost a nickel, but I didn't care because this would be my first ride on a tow. I'd never skied down a slope I hadn't climbed."

Born in 1903 in Potsdam, New York, he began a journalism career as a part-time copy boy at the Parliamentary Press Gallery in Ottawa, Canada, where his father was a newspaper correspondent. His mother was from Switzerland, and it was there that Berry first tasted the fun of gliding over snow. During one trip across the Atlantic to return to preparatory school, the self-assured nine-year-old wrote a description of icebergs. His story was published by the *Ottawa Journal* as a sidebar for its coverage on the sinking of the Titanic.

By 1927 he was writing for the *New York Tribune* and assigned to cover Charles Lindbergh's solo transatlantic flight. "I stood beside Lindy, and I remember how his lips shook just before he climbed into the plane."

Stirred with the spirit of adventure, Berry was soon ready to see the West. "I took Horace Greeley to heart. I'd first flown over Reno and the Sierra Nevada, and it looked like a nice place to raise a family." He began as a full-time linotype operator for the *Nevada State Journal* in 1928 and freelanced for New York newspapers as a correspondent covering celebrities seeking quick divorces and marriages in Reno. Occasionally, he slipped in stories about Western skiing and lifestyles in his weekly dispatches.

"In 1935 C.J. Lilley, publisher of the *Sacramento Union*, was reading some of my stuff. He asked me if I thought this sport of skiing was going anywhere. I said 'Hell, yes!'" Lilley hired Berry as a ski columnist for $15 a week. Other newspapers like the *Sacramento Bee, Los Angeles Mirror, New York Times* and *San Francisco Examiner* assigned Berry to cover the 1932 Olympic Trials in Tahoe City, the 1950 F.I.S. World Championships at Aspen, the 1960 Winter Olympics at Squaw Valley and other events.

"Skiing changed everything in the Sierra loop. It developed the mountains. And it was fun. I couldn't believe I was getting paid to do it."

In the early 1930s Bill Berry cofounded the California Ski Association and helped organize the Reno Ski Club. In 1933 he climbed Galena Creek to Mount Rose with Jim Crawford and Wayne Poulsen in search of a ski area site. Six years later he returned to ride Nevada's first rope tow at

Shoe boxes stuffed with photo negatives, media badges and race bibs, and cartons overflowing with newspaper clippings fill Bill Berry's office in his Reno home where he's lived since 1940. Two of Berry's most prized possessions are the Saint Olaf medal bestowed upon him by the King of Norway and his book, Lost Sierra.

© *Carolyn Caddes*

"My second day out here in December (1928), I traveled to Truckee and the ski area at Hilltop. I rented a pair of skis made of pine. Beyond the lodge stood the lower terminal of an amazing contraption known locally as a pullback. It was, at the moment, the only ski tow in America. On the right of the slope they had a ski jump. You could tell almost immediately the jumpers were pretty clannish. However, my first trip I sailed off it 50 feet and immediately became one of the boys."

Mount Rose Upski. He was on Donner Summit to ride the West's first chairlift at Sugar Bowl the day it opened in 1939.

Over the years, as Berry chronicled Western skiing's celebrated events, he also collected historical ski artifacts that could illustrate his stories. In 1976, with the help of the Sons of Norway and the Auburn Ski Club, he founded the William B. Berry Western America Skisport Museum at Boreal at Donner Pass. The majority of irreplaceable exhibits that he accumulated remain an incredible resource for recounting and preserving the history of skiing in North America.

While his longtime association with Wendell Robie, founder of Auburn Ski Club, was vital in development of the museum, it was a turbulent relationship, Berry admits. "I've never been paid so little by anyone for so much work!" Their unabating differences of opinion eventually led to the removal of Berry's name and association from the museum.

Fifteen years later, however, the Auburn Ski Club agreed to finance *Lost Sierra: Gold, Ghosts & Skis*, a book authored by Bill Berry and edited by Chapman Wentworth about the origins of skiing in the northern Sierra Nevada published in 1991. The idea began when Berry traveled to Plumas County in 1931 to help a local newspaper editor with linotype over a busy weekend. "I stopped at a place called Four Hills Mine and saw a pair of 16-foot longboards hanging on the wall. I was curious and began to talk to Lemon O'Rourke about the skis. Then I interviewed more of the old miners who had artifacts and notes about 'snowshoe' racing for gold. I started doing a few stories, then ran a piece in the *National Geographic* on the subject which by then I'd named *Lost Sierra*."

Longboard racers of La Porte, whose story Bill Berry tells in his book, Lost Sierra.

Bill Berry was elected to the U.S. National Ski Hall of Fame and honored with a Lifetime Achievement Award from the International Skiing History Association. At the reception Bill Berry told the crowd, "Actually, I have to admit that journalism was my vocation, skiing just my avocation. You see, I was bit by the virus years ago."

Courtesy of William B. Berry

*After receiving the Saint Olaf medal from King Olaf of Norway
for his lifetime support of international skiing
and an honorary membership in the Sons of Norway,
Bill Berry presented the king with a U.S.S.A. plaque.*

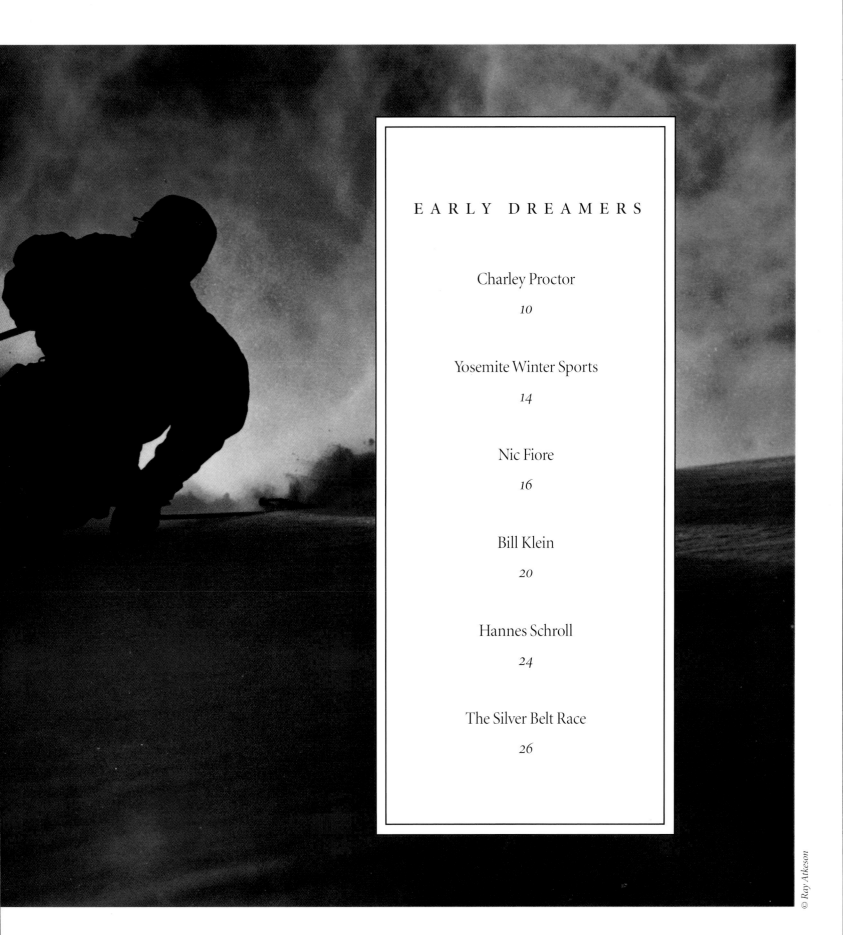

EARLY DREAMERS

CHARLEY
PROCTOR
—
YOSEMITE
NATIONAL
PARK

1906 – 1996

*The North American
Ski Journalists Association
established an award in
Proctor's name to honor
others who have made
significant contributions
to the sport of skiing.*

harley Proctor arrived with his young family in Yosemite Valley in 1938, far from New England where he was raised and educated. Son of a physics professor at Dartmouth College who had set the first ski slalom course in North America, Proctor was a well-educated and accomplished skier.

Assured and graceful on snow, Charley Proctor had challenged slopes considered unskiable by most. He was the first to schuss Tuckerman's Ravine, a 1000-foot drop down a fifty-five degree slope on New Hampshire's 6,288-foot Mount Washington.

As an intercollegiate jumping champion at Dartmouth, he had captained the ski team in 1927 and 1928. He pitted his skills against the world's best as a member of the U.S. Olympic Team in the 1928 Saint Moritz Winter Games, competing in ski jumping and cross-country. That same year he was the first American to race in the inaugural Arlberg-Kandahar in St. Anton, Austria.

Proctor laid out ski trails at Pico Peak in Vermont and Pinkam Notch in New Hampshire and directed the design of ski trails for the U.S. Forest Service in other Eastern states. From 1935 to 1937 he coached the Harvard ski team and wrote two books on skiing.

Don Tresidder, president of Yosemite Park & Curry Company, met the quiet, young man who was on a business trip to California. They agreed to ski together at Badger Pass, after which Tresidder invited Proctor to move to the West to become the director of Yosemite's winter sports program.

Although the ski industry was still in its infancy, Badger Pass, with the addition of its first lift, was becoming popular with the social elite, which was no problem for the Dartmouth grad, who was seldom seen without his trademark cap. "We liked Yosemite and the people liked us," he recalled in his journal. "They wanted us to stay, and the company gave me a job as assistant supervisor of all stores and gift shops. We drove back East and sold our house."

He was considered America's foremost authority on skiing in 1940, examining the skills of the best instructors in the country who were being certified. "His focus was the development of the sport," remembers his daughter, Peggy Dean, who was born in Yosemite. "And skiing itself remained his passion. He did a lot of exploring throughout the park, in Tuolumne and on Mount Hoffman."

He worked closely with the Tresidders in improving the runs and exploring the area for the site of the soon to be constructed Ostrander Hut. Proctor's passion and immense joy for skiing can be discovered in a passage he wrote about touring near Ostrander Lake with Mary Tresidder. "She loved the mountains and enjoyed being in them. Her skiing was a means to this end, not an end in itself as it is to many. When we found a beautiful long slope of perfect spring snow or light powder, she would ski it with obvious pleasure and was enthusiastic, but always seemed to express her feelings in her quiet way."

Historical photo courtesy of Peggy Dean

"When Charley left Yosemite, he was almost seventy, and he was still about the prettiest skier on the slope.
He had such style and grace. It didn't look like it took any effort at all,"
said Anne Hendrickson, president of the Far West Ski Association.

It was a comfortable place to live and work for Charley Proctor and his family. "The guests who came to Yosemite to ski were, in a way, comparable to the skiers we had left behind back East," he wrote. "They were the socially prominent leaders in the business world: back East from Boston, and here, from San Francisco; back East, Harvard students, and in Yosemite, Stanford and Cal graduates."

He became the first secretary for the California Ski Association and its vice president when the organization was renamed the Far West Ski Association. In 1958 he was appointed as a member of the Squaw Valley Winter Olympic Ski Advisory Committee and elected a member of the U.S. National Ski Hall of Fame.

Courtesy of Sandy Poulsen

Under Charley Proctor's guidance, Yosemite kept pace with the ever-growing winter parade of outdoor enthusiasts.
By the start of World War II, Badger Pass was hosting more than 73,000 visitors during winter months,
up from 30,000 in 1935. Pictured here is Wayne Poulsen in a jumping event during the 1930s.

Bill, Mary, Charley, Peggy and Nancy Proctor in Yosemite, 1953.
"Skiing itself remained his passion," says Peggy Dean of her father whom she knew as a kind, gentle and loving man.
"Though he was well known in the ski world for his dedication and promotion of the sport,
he remained very unassuming and modest." Charley Proctor promoted skiing in Yosemite until 1971
and remained devoted to the sport until his death in 1996 at age ninety.

Famed ski expert, Jules Frisch, came to Yosemite in 1928 to direct the ski school. Here he is on Indian Ridge overlooking the high country.

Courtesy of the National Park Service, Yosemite

Yosemite became a national park in 1890; however, it wasn't until Congress created the National Park Service in 1916 that supervised winter activities took place within the park.

Yosemite Park & Curry Company, park concessionaire, established the Yosemite Winter Club in 1928 "to encourage the development of all forms of winter sports." Horace Albright, the club's first director, and Don Tresidder, president of the Curry Company, hired Ernest des Baillets, famous French-Swiss snow sports expert, to direct the development of winter sports in the park. They created a small ski hill and ski jump near Tenaya Creek Bridge and organized a ski school under Jules Frisch. He and Gordon Hooley (future general manager of Sugar Bowl), Wolf Greeven and Swiss skier-skater Ralph de Pfyffer led ski tours with instruction to such destinations as Mount Watkins, Snow Flat and Tenaya Lake.

The opening of Wawona Road and Tunnel in 1934 and Glacier Point Road to Badger Pass in 1935 made it possible to build a ski lodge 23 miles from Yosemite Valley at Monroe Meadows. With a summit elevation of 8,000 feet and a vertical drop of 800 feet, Badger Pass was welcoming 30,000 skiers annually by 1935.

The West's first mechanical lift, known as the "Upski," carried six persons at a time up 280 vertical feet. In 1936 it was extended to Ski-Top, where Badger's famed Rail, Bishop and Strawberry Creek runs were cleared. In publicizing Yosemite, Tresidder claimed that Badger Pass slopes were "as good as the most famous runs in the Swiss Alps or Austrian Tyrol."

Some instructors who were at Badger Pass from the beginning moved on to pioneer skiing at the West's best-known ski resorts: Sigi Engl went to Sun Valley; Hannes Schroll to Sugar Bowl; and Luggi Foeger to Donner Summit and Lake Tahoe to run the ski schools at Sugar Bowl and Alpine Meadows.

Courtesy of the National Park Service, Yosemite

Luggi Foeger carving a christie in the powder snow.

Hannes Schroll with two skiers at Badger Pass in 1938.

Bill Klein and Luggi Foeger relax at Badger Pass races. Bill Klein was at Sugar Bowl and Luggi was head of the ski school at Badger Pass.

Yosemite's Upski, the West's first mechanical lift, nicknamed the "Queen Mary," took skiers to the famed Rail Creek, Bishop and Strawberry Creek runs in 1936.

*"A deep strength emerges
from being in the mountains.
You're in sync with nature, and
that gives you an inner strength.
I'm going to pull all stops
in the world. I hope that
I'll never be in a rest home.
I'm going to keep on going."*

ic Fiore first arrived in Yosemite Valley in December 1948. "For myself it was a culture shock. I didn't speak the language too well. I said, 'What's going to happen?' I almost chickened out."

"Luggi hadn't been able to pick us up at the train station in Merced until 7:30 in the evening. I was studying the palm trees. That was the first time I'd seen palm trees. I say, 'Gee, boys, I wonder where we're going.' We waited and finally he arrives."

It began snowing hard. The twenty-eight-year-old French Canadian skier and his Canadian friends helped Luggi Foeger, Badger Pass ski school director, put tire chains on the 1946 Ford sedan in Mariposa. Entering the valley, huge snow flakes fell past unseen granite walls that loomed 3,000 feet above.

"We came in here at night, really tired, went to bed, woke up the next morning. I'd never see so much snow. I was looking around because I didn't have the least idea that we need to drive 23 miles to Badger Pass. I was looking up at Yosemite Falls and I said, 'Where in the world do the beginners ski?' I'd never seen a sky so blue. And the sun. It just hit me like a bolt of lightning to see this place."

His journey from Montréal to Yosemite began when he was eight years old. "Somebody gave me a pair of skis. They were huge, 200 centimeters. I went to the mountains in the Laurentians. You paid twenty-five cents to take the train. You saved. Your allowance was ten cents a week. I mean, I come from a family of twelve children. My mother was widowed when I was six years old. You really saved so that you can ski. Once I got on my skis, there was no holding back. I became totally crazy, insane and committed about skiing."

A physical education instructor in the Canadian army during World War II, Fiore skied every chance he could. After his release from the army in 1946, he passed his Canadian Ski Instructors Certification and settled at the Saint Adele Lodge in the Laurentians as a ski instructor and summer sports director. There, the amiable instructor met Luggi Foeger, famed Uber-patriarch of ski instruction.

Foeger, always on the lookout for new talent, asked Fiore to return with him to Yosemite. "I only came for one winter because I wanted to go back to college. I had so many big plans, and I didn't speak English, coming from Canada. I was strictly educated in the French language. When I first arrived, I knew I'd fallen in love with Yosemite. I just didn't want to admit it."

"The first time I skied at Badger we went down Rail Creek. That used to be a national course. It's about six miles and over 2,000 vertical feet. We went down that powder, up to here, and I'll tell you, I'd never seen powder like that. We took a few somersaults. We came back and Luggi said, 'All of you, you skied like pigs, absolutely like pigs!' He was very serious about skiing. And when Luggi said something, that was the gospel, the pope of skiing. So, that night we got together, the guys who come with me from Canada, Ross Moore, Jim McConkey. I said, 'Boys, we better get to work.'"

© Carolyn Caddes

Pedaling his bike through Wawona Tunnel his first summer at Yosemite, Nic was chased by an irate park ranger in his truck.
"I didn't know the siren was for me. I didn't understand English, see, and the only bike I owned was a track bike with a fixed gear.
You put your hand on the front tire to stop. It took me ten miles to stop. Gee, I was going really fast."

Work he did. Under Foeger's tutelage Fiore earned his certification in ski instruction in March 1949 at the old Strawberry Resort on Highway 50. "I still remember my examiners, Luggi Foeger, Hannes Schroll, Otto Steiner, Charley Proctor, Corty Hill, Tommy Tindel and Sepp Benedikter."

Nic setting poles for a race in 1969.

Courtesy of Nic Fiore

Foeger coached him into becoming an accomplished skier and preached a commitment to the sport. "For my first twenty years of teaching, and I'm not exaggerating, I skied seven days a week. I could never get enough. I was very serious at it. I was taught that you make a commitment, and, gee, that's what it is. To Luggi there was only one way to do it, but perfect. With him we were always at our best, trying to do the very, very best."

Fiore was often asked if he ever thought of moving on to a more glamorous ski area. "Obviously, with the park system, Badger could never expand. I always knew the terrain here could never compete with Sun Valley. How can a small area compete? My answer, I say, 'Come to Yosemite. We have a ski school which really teaches people to ski and focuses on beginner and family. You can have a really lovely day here.'"

When Nic Fiore replaced Foeger in 1958, he changed things. "Luggi taught Arlberg Technique, a lot of wind-up and follow-through with a lot of rotation. You never spoke of the feet for turning. What I did was start telling people that the turn is initiated from the feet. I had tremendous results. Then I just cut down the amount of wind-up and follow-through. It was just a slight wind-up and delayed rotation. Basically, I tried to keep it simple. No student should be burdened with a lot of technical jargon. Let them enjoy themselves, and let them ski."

A combination of modernized ski equipment, Fiore's modified Arlberg system and a simplified approach to teaching skiing created immediate results, especially with children. Author of an instructional book called *So You Want To Ski?*, he began one of the first children's ski programs in the country. "I had a hard time getting it off the ground. A lot of ski teachers didn't want to be bothered teaching children, but I pushed it."

Today, the Badger Pass Pups Program for preschoolers is extremely successful. "People were satisfied and the ski school grew and grew. As a matter of fact, it ended up we were giving seven, eight, nine hundred lessons a day. I didn't have enough ski teachers." It's estimated that the spirited Fiore has taught nearly 100,000 people to ski. In forty-nine years of teaching, Fiore didn't miss a day of work until an on-hill accident at Badger Pass in 1995 resulted in a broken ankle.

He has been involved more than forty-five years in the Professional Ski Instructors of America and served as an officer, director and examiner. In 1971 the organization voted him as the year's most valuable ski instructor.

The North American Ski Journalists Association presented Fiore with the prestigious Charley Proctor Award in 1986, and the following year he was elected to the U.S. National Ski Hall of Fame.

His *joie de vivre* is apparent in his endless stories about life in Yosemite. He smiles, hums a song and admits, "It gets a little harder. The aches and pains won't go away, but, gee, it's better to die walking, or doing a little bit of nordic, than in a rocking chair."

"The ski industry has changed, the competition has changed,
but the one thing that hasn't changed is
the thrill of getting someone to make their first run.
I don't think that thrill will ever diminish."

*"We went to the very top
of the summit and looked
down to Donner Lake.
We saw nothing but these
big boulders of granite.
I said, 'My God,
where do people ski?'
We couldn't believe it,
because in Austria we never
got that much snow.
It was hard for us
to visualize beautiful slopes.
We had no idea."*

t was summer 1936. Bill Klein, an accomplished skier and just nineteen, arrived at Donner Summit with his brother Fred at the invitation of Dr. Joel Hildebrand who assured the skeptical, young Austrians that by winter everything would be covered with snow. Hildebrand, manager of the U.S. Olympic Alpine Team and president of the Sierra Club, had met the Klein brothers in Austria and persuaded them to come to California to open their own ski school near the Sierra Club's Clair Tappaan Lodge.

During the drive west, the Kleins visited fellow Austrian and ski school director Hans Hauser at Sun Valley who offered them a job, Bill Klein remembers. "Hauser said, 'Why don't you just stay with me right here?' He was going to have eight instructors in Sun Valley. At that time, it was probably a lot." They were also offered jobs at Mount Rainier, but the Kleins were committed to their promise to Dr. Hildebrand.

"I never wanted to work for someone else. My instincts were to advance myself. Though Donner Summit wasn't acclaimed like a Sun Valley, we had the opportunity to establish our own ski school."

Once in California, they paid a visit to Austrian Hannes Schroll, director of the Badger Pass Ski School in Yosemite. "Hannes would like to have us stay right there. He thought we were kind of an asset because, at that time, my brother played the guitar, and we sang and yodeled and entertained the people. But we said we were going to the Donner Summit area. He said, 'Oh, Donner Summit, I don't think there's any skiing up there.'"

The brothers opened Ski School Klein in the winter of 1936. Their students were mostly San Franciscans and other Bay Area visitors who stayed at Rainbow Lodge or Soda Springs. "We would take them up to Mount Lincoln before there was ever a Sugar Bowl. To them, especially with all the hiking we had to do, our ski lessons were all very novel and something fun."

Bill Klein was born Wilhelm Klein in Traisen Lilienfeld in the lower Austrian Alps in February 1917. "Skiing was my lifeblood. I began schussing before I was five years old." Klein skied competitively while in school and won the prestigious Grossglockner Race in Austria in his early teens. He also began teaching skiing at a young age. As a boy he took lessons from legendary ski instructor Mathias Zdarsky who developed an innovative ski technique using a stem turn based on the single-pole Norwegian telemark style.

"Zdarsky was kind of a peculiar fellow, very entrenched in his method. He didn't accept anybody else's new ideas. One year I learned the Arlberg method from an instructor who'd just returned from being certified in the two-pole, Schneider technique. Although Zdarsky was a close friend of my family, when he saw me skiing with two poles, he didn't allow me to ski on his ski slopes where he taught anymore. He thought that we betrayed him. A sensitive man he was."

A year after opening their ski school, the area around Mount Lincoln was up for sale. "The land was owned by two sisters in Sacramento who leased out the property for sheep grazing.

© Carolyn Caddes

"There's a satisfaction knowing I was part of developing the sport from my childhood to what it is now.
It's just something I enjoyed the moment I stepped into my skis.
Seventy years skiing, oh boy. That's enough for anyone!"

They offered me close to 700 acres around Mount Lincoln for $2,000. I just didn't have the money. However, I told Hannes about Donner Summit and the Sugar Bowl. He says, there's only one place in California, and that's Yosemite, of course. He never had seen the Sugar Bowl until we brought him up there."

Klein took Schroll and Dr. Otto Barkan, a prominent eye surgeon from Stanford, on a tour. "Hannes immediately recognized the possibilities. We walked up Nob Hill and already he's saying, 'We can build a golf course here and in the summer have cows grazing there.' All kinds of visions right away. He had all the right connections from teaching a number of affluent businessmen from San Francisco while directing the Badger Pass Ski School. I was very happy for him."

Schroll and a group of investors bought land on Donner Summit for $6,750 in 1938. Schroll became president of the new Sugar Bowl Corporation and offered Klein the position of ski school director. "It would have meant working under someone else, even if it was Hannes, so I decided to stay at the Sierra Club. Hannes allowed my ski school access to the mountain so it worked out okay."

Klein's ski school advocated the Arlberg "American" technique and was soon considered one of the best in the country. He developed his own style, which advocated a closed parallel stance rather than the stemming method taught in the Arlberg technique. Although his mentors would have been appalled, it worked, and he became a trendsetter. Bill Klein coached the champion University of California, Berkeley ski team in 1939 and 1940, and competed in F.I.S. races. He also founded the California Ski Instructors Association, along with Schroll, Hildebrand, Otto Steiner, Corty Hill and Luggi Foeger.

Sugar Bowl opened with the first chairlift in the Sierra Nevada in December 1939. During World War II , like most of the skilled instructors at ski resorts across the country, Bill Klein joined the U.S. Army's Tenth Mountain Division to train new ski instructors. It wasn't until after the war that he finally agreed to direct the Sugar Bowl ski school.

"Sugar Bowl wanted me to become the general manager after the war. I really wasn't that interested. My instincts were to get into retail. I saw my future in a ski shop. Skiing was quickly becoming fashionable, and many people were taking it up. I could teach, own my own store, and still be my own boss."

Bill Klein returned frequently to Austria to visit, but it would never again be home. "You know, when you've lived in the United States, everything changes. I would never be able to live in Austria again. It is too small for me. The country is beautiful and people are nice, but your whole activity, it's too limited. We never would have had opportunities in Austria like we had here, that I was able to get involved in sporting goods and retailing, then real estate. Those opportunities, you don't have in Europe."

Courtesy of Robert Frohlich

Bill Klein doing a Geländesprung.

Klein fulfilled his dream in 1945, when he opened Klein's Ski Shop, one of the first ski shops in the Sierra Nevada, near the bottom terminal of Sugar Bowl's Mount Disney lift. It was fellow Tenth Mountain Division soldier, Hans Hagemeister, who brought innovative products from Europe—Alu metal skis, Bogner stretch pants and Henke buckle-on boots—to sell in Klein's shop.

"I was responsible for Hans getting the Bogner line. I knew Willi Bogner quite well. He wanted me to be his importer, but I just didn't want to get involved. I didn't like traveling. I had my ski school and ski shop. In the summers, Fred and I had a real estate business in the Bay Area. Hans did a great job, however, introducing Bogner to the American public."

In the 1950s, Howard Head, a former aviation engineer who developed the first-ever metal-bonded ski, asked Klein to be one of his chief ski testers. Klein accepted but declined a partnership offer in Head's company to remain a ski instructor. It was a decision he later regretted. "Every time I ran into Howard years later at Sun Valley, he'd tease me. With a $60,000 investment he and his partners cashed out for nine million. Isn't that something?"

It was also then that he met his second wife. German-born Anneliese was taking a ski lesson, struggling in heavy snow, when she saw a man skiing "like a knife cutting through butter." She asked her instructor to introduce her to the powerful, elegant skier whom she eventually married.

As he became more involved in his ski shops at Sugar Bowl, in Berkeley and in San Francisco, Klein retired from ski teaching, although his method of instruction continued to influence others. The Professional Ski Instructors of America honored him with their Lifetime Achievement Award, and in 1996 the North American Ski Journalists Association presented him with the Charley Proctor Award for his significant contribution to the sport.

Ski School Klein at Sugar Bowl in the late 1940s.

"When I think back, it was a wonderful life, to see the winter sport develop the way it did in California. It's amazing how many people have gone into the sport. Skiing is changing somewhat. The younger generation, they're all going into snowboarding. I'm just wondering how long they're going to be able to do it. You can ski as long as you can walk, but I question if a seventy-five-year-old man or woman can snowboard. It's an interesting thought."

"I arrived in America with twenty-five dollars in my pocket, holes in my pants, skis on my back and not able to speak a word of English, yet I was still able to see my dreams come true."

Hannes Schroll was twenty-eight when he was invited by fellow Austrian Bill Klein to look at a future ski area on Donner Summit in 1938. Schroll was ambitious and self-reliant, and, in the years to come, he would display the same tenacity and dedication in operating Sugar Bowl that he had as a ski racer.

Encouraged by his father, Schroll learned to ski in the small Tyrolean hamlet where he was born. When he won his first race, his prize was a pair of real hickory skis to replace the barrel staves his father had fashioned for him. "Stick to your skiing," his father told him. "Some day Austria will be proud of you."

Schroll won more than 100 international ski titles in Europe. In 1934 he earned the nickname "Red Devil of Tyrol" when he captured the hair-raising Marmolata Race in the Italian Alps, then known as the fastest downhill in the world. The following year, he was honored by Chancellor Kurt von Schuschnigg to represent Austria at the first Federation International du Ski (F.I.S.) championship held in the Pacific Northwest.

It was there that Schroll, the "man without fear" with a perpetual grin, was spotted by Yosemite's Don and Mary Tresidder. Racing through clouds that had settled on the Mount Rainier course, Schroll easily skied and yodeled his way to victory in both slalom and downhill. The Tresidders saw the need for a colorful skier like Schroll at Badger Pass and helped him secure immigration status by appointing him director of the ski school.

He stayed in Yosemite for two years before leaving to devote his full time to the development of Sugar Bowl. By October 1938, Schroll was named president of the new Sugar Bowl Corporation, and within a year he would secure the future of the resort by persuading Walt Disney to become the resort's first substantial stockholder. Disney's $5,000 check started a mild flurry of stock buying by prominent ski enthusiasts and wealthy businessmen living in the San Francisco Bay Area. The investors included W. W. Crocker, president of Crocker Bank, architect William Wurster, who designed the original four-story wooden lodge named "Le Grand Hotel," and Jerome Hill, grandson of the founder of the Great Northern Railroad. Hill later pushed for the construction of the Magic Carpet gondola. Schroll's commitment to Sugar Bowl was assured when he fell in love with and married Hill's sister Maud.

"Skiing was my father's life-consuming passion," said his son, Chris Schroll. "He won races into the 1950s, afterwards always yodeling to the bar. He did so much to help skiing grow into the tremendous sport that it is today. Sugar Bowl, however, remained his proudest accomplishment."

Hannes stepped down as Sugar Bowl's corporate president in 1945 but remained associated with the ski area for the rest of his life. Although he skied for another twenty years, he moved out of the mountains to Hollister where he raised cattle and bred race horses until his death in 1985 at the age of seventy-six. A member of the World Ski Hall of Fame, Hannes Schroll was inducted into the U.S. National Ski Hall of Fame in 1966.

Photograph by Ansel Adams

*"You are so stiff, you stand like a Christmas tree!" was Hannes Schroll's frequent comment
as a ski instructor. "My student, you will have to bend your knees some day,
why not save my time by doing it now?"*

Top international ski racers traveled each spring to the Tyrolean-like resort on Donner Summit to compete in a giant slalom race that began atop Mount Lincoln. The Silver Belt race course at Sugar Bowl took skiers straight down the mountain's steep side into a large gully and finally into a sheltered natural basin. Early winners of this premier skiing event took home the coveted silver-studded belt with a silver buckle.

Bill Klein, the resort's ski school director who set the race course in the 1940s and 1950s, says, "It was one of the most natural giant slalom courses anywhere."

Toni Marth, a former Sugar Bowl ski school director, set the course for its last fifteen years. "It took courage, ability, strength and endurance to run it. It was very technical, where the racer could reach high speeds banking his turns from one side of the gully to the other."

Don Schwartz, president of Sugar Bowl for twenty years, recalls the race with pride. "One could easily equate it to today's World Cup. All the champions and stars of the day participated."

The list of Silver Belt winners reads like a skiing Hall of Fame. Sun Valley Ski School Director, Friedl Pfeifer, won the first men's race in 1940. Gretchen Fraser, the first American to win an Olympic alpine medal, won the women's. Two more Olympic medalists, Greg Jones and Cindy Nelson, won the last competition in 1975. In between, the winners were equally prominent: Christian Pravda in 1953; Buddy Werner in 1959 and 1962; Leo Lacroix in 1964; Starr Walton in 1957 and 1960; Jean Saubert in 1963 and 1965.

Although participants and race officials agree that the Silver Belt was one of the most challenging races of its time, it was the atmosphere of the race itself that stands out in their memories.

Since there was no road access to the ski hill, all of the racers stayed at the resort. "The fact that it was so small and cozy made it easy for the skiers to get to know one another," says Schwartz.

The same coziness, however, was also one of the causes for its demise. With the formation of the World Cup in 1967, the Silver Belt lost some of its prestige. When the World Cup races were held at Heavenly from 1972 to 1974, the Silver Belt was cancelled. The 30th Annual and last official race was held in 1975.

Courtesy of Babette Haueisen

*"It was a wonderful race,"
recalled the late
Sally Neidlinger Hudson, a 1952
U.S. Olympic Team member
from New Hampshire
who won the Belt in 1953.
"Coming to California for
a week in the spring was
a real attraction.
There was a camaraderie
among all the racers and
everyone was in a good mood."
Here she is at the top of the
course. Notice that this is
before any lift to the top of
Mount Lincoln.*

Gretchen Fraser, 1940

Alf Engen, 1946

Brynhild Graesmoen, 1948

Courtesy of Sugar Bowl

*Greg Jones and Cindy
Nelson, 1975. Winners of the
last official Silver Belt.*

Courtesy of the Auburn Ski Club

Tom Corcoran and Starr Walton, 1960

1940
Friedl Pfeifer
Gretchen Fraser

1941
Chris Schwarzenbach
Clarita Heath

1942
Chris Schwarzenbach
Kaki Henck

1943–1945
Cancelled due to
WW II

1946
Alf Engen
Rhoda Wurtele

1947
Kristofer Berg
Ann Volkmann

1948
George Macomber
Brynhild Graesmoen

1949
Yves Latreille
Dodie Post

1950
Guttorm Berge
Jannette Burr

1951
Guttorm Berge
Sally Neidlinger

1952
Yvan Tache
Mary Jane Griffith

1953
Christian Pravda
Janette Burr

1954
John Cress
Bamse Woronovsky

1955
Bill Beck
Babette Haueisen

1956
Christian Pravda
Sally Deaver

1957
Christian Pravda
Starr Walton

1958
Kenny Lloyd
Cathy Zimmermann

1959
Buddy Werner
Linda Meyers

1960
Tom Corcoran
Starr Walton

1961
Chuck Ferries
Linda Meyers

1962
Buddy Werner
Linda Meyers

1963
Willy Favre
Jean Saubert

1964
Leo Lacroix
Pia Riva

1965
Rod Hebron
Jean Saubert

1966
Philippe Mollard
Kathy Allen

1967
Scott Henderson
Lee Hall

1968
Rick Chaffee
Marilyn Cochran

1969
Eric Poulsen
Barbara Cochran

1970
Eric Poulsen
Marilyn Cochran

1971
Pat Simpson
Cheryl Bechdolt

1972–1974
No races

1975
Greg Jones
Cindy Nelson

Above Mammoth Mountain.

BIG DREAMS

© *Tom Lippert*

DAVE McCOY

—

MAMMOTH MOUNTAIN

"I fell in love with the area the first time I saw it in 1926. I loved the snow more than anything in those mountains. It reminded me of diamonds as the sun sparkled off it. I just felt magnetized, drawn. There was some power I can't explain. The most important thing was to get here."

t age twelve, while on a trip with his mother, Dave McCoy stopped briefly in Bishop, California. Its impressive surrounding landscape took hold of him. He knew he would return. Six years later, when he was eighteen, he tied his skis on the back of his Harley Davidson at his home in Washington and rode south to the Owens Valley on the east side of the Sierra Nevada.

McCoy got a job as a mechanic and dishwasher in the small town of Independence. "Every chance I got I'd lash my skis to the back of the Harley and head to the slopes with a ski buddy." His ski buddy also had a sister named Roma, a beautiful, seventeen-year-old high school cheerleader who worked part-time as a bank clerk.

Skiing was everything to McCoy who was willing to hock his motorcycle in 1938 to buy a portable rope tow. "It was hard to convince the bank to give me $85 for it." Enchanted by the ambitious boy friend, Roma convinced the bank to grant him the loan and threatened to quit her job if they didn't. "That's the God's truth!" It also convinced McCoy that this was the woman he wanted to marry.

Three years later, the U.S. Forest Service granted him a permit for a roving rope tow. He set it up wherever the snow pack was best—at Dead Man Summit, Onion Valley or McGee's—and invited people to join in the fun, never charging them until one day, approaching poverty, he asked for donations. "We made $15 the first time, enough to pay for expenses and dinner for both of us. I thought, this might turn into a pretty good business."

Working outside where he loved to play was his primary goal. "I just loved the outdoors. I always fished and hiked in the early years. I'd go by myself overnight. I still like that." He met a hydrographer in Independence whose job it was to measure streams and gauge snow depth. "I said, that's what I want to do; this is where I want to get my foothold. I was brought here to do something, and there were steps put in front of me. Nothing else interfered."

Waiting for an opportunity to take the hydrographer's civil service exam, he worked as a cement finisher and surveyor while ski racing in the winter. His friend Corty Hill, a Badger Pass ski racer and grandson of Great Northern Railway baron James Hill, coached McCoy, who became a formidable ski racer and won the California State Championship in 1941. The next year, however, during the state championships at Sugar Bowl, he suffered serious injuries in a fall that ended his competitive skiing career but did not keep him off the slopes.

Fortunately, the mountains offered McCoy another opportunity. When three feet of snow blanketed the Owens Valley floor, hydrographers couldn't get in. They sent their protégé, the powerful young skier who found it natural to be doing his job on skis. McCoy went on to earn the top grade on the civil service exam out of a field of four hundred applicants. Soon after, he was offered a full-time job as a hydrographer in Crowley, a small town a few miles south of Mammoth, which is exactly where he wanted to be.

"Skiing to me is life itself. There is great strength in the mountains.
To be able to ski and to be lucky enough to be in the mountains is a revitalization."

On his regular trips into the mountains to measure snow depths, McCoy noticed that the broad shoulders of a dormant volcano just west of Mammoth Lakes funneled Pacific storms over its 11,000-foot crest, dropping heavy snow on the wide-open bowls. "It looked like the best skiing I'd ever seen. The slopes were pitched right. I knew God had made this place to be a ski mountain."

The U.S. Forest Service had hired Luggi Foeger, Hannes Schneider and Corty Hill as consultants to look for new ski area terrain in the West. "They chartered a DC-3 and flew the entire coast to Vancouver looking at all the mountains for development. They stopped here, too. They said that the mountain was too high, it got too much snow, and it was too far from a major population area."

Courtesy of Mammoth Mountain

Young Dave McCoy surveys his first lodge as skiers prepare for a spring day on the slopes in the late 40s.

McCoy set out to prove them wrong. He installed the first permanent rope tow on the north side of Mammoth Mountain in 1945 and two years later constructed a small day lodge. In 1953, he drove his wife to the base of the mountain. He said, "I quit my job. I can't do two things at once, and I want to do one thing really well. I want to work at building Mammoth Mountain into a ski area where lots of people can come and have fun."

The U.S. Forest Service solicited bids for the ski area site. With no money, a wife and six kids to support, McCoy needed a plan. "I took a piece of paper and said, here's where Rope Tow One is," pointing to his rough sketch of the mountain. "We will build a chairlift here and one here and another one there. I think we can do that." In 1954 McCoy received a twenty-five-year use permit under the condition that he begin to develop the mountain.

By the mid-50s Mammoth was attracting more skiers than any other California operation, including Sugar Bowl and Badger Pass at Yosemite. Skiers willingly drove 350 miles from Los Angeles. "It grew by demand. Now you don't have that luxury of saying demand is enough for expansion." In 1955 Dave and his workers installed Mammoth's first double chairlift, mixing the cement, digging tower holes and building the drive system. "It took us all. Every time I needed someone to do a specific job, he was delivered to me."

McCoy sees Mammoth Mountain as a prep school for life. "We figure that we owe something to the kids that come here to work. It's an introduction to what life is about. We teach them all we can about working with people, and people skills is one of the most important things to learn. Through the years, the kids that have come here have learned, gone to work and come back to say what a great start in life it was."

Ninety-five percent of McCoy's time is spent talking with people. That skill was most important when Mammoth was threatened by the dry years of the mid-70s. He was forced to reorganize his company and let valuable people go. "I had a big loan out to begin with, and the bank wanted to foreclose. We did have to cut back, and that was probably the hardest time of my life in business, to see capable people let go, people that I could use. I never doubted we were going forward. That's what sold the bank. We would have been out of business in a minute if we couldn't sell ourselves. They gave us one year to do it, and we outdid ourselves. That's the year we put in all the snowmaking and talked them into giving us money instead of cutting us off. They gave us another start. Everything could be rated a disaster if you don't take it on as a challenge, something to overcome, right then. We did, and we learned, and we always went forward."

McCoy and Mammoth Mountain employees have also supported their community. There were only six people living year-round in Mammoth in 1952 when McCoy bought a snowplow to provide winter access to the village. "As we saw the real demanding needs, such as water, some of the employees here started the first water district. Some of them helped start the volunteer fire department. We needed a hospital, so we started in on it; I worked eighteen years on the hospital board. When it became evident that we needed a high school, we got the votes for that. We needed a college to educate the people who come here to work, even adults, so they can further their education to make their next step in life." His community college project began six years ago, and classes are now in session. Planning for expansion to a four-year college has begun.

Sixty years after Dave McCoy first climbed Mammoth Mountain on skis, he still believes in the power of the mountains. "Everybody sacrifices or feels that they sacrifice to live in the mountains. Your jobs aren't as glorious, your income isn't so big and the cost of living's a little higher, but I think, when it's all said and done, you've sacrificed for sanity, health and a good life. It really turns out you're ahead of the game."

Courtesy of Mammoth Mountain

Rope tow #2 in 1950.

Gary, Roma and Dave McCoy in 1950.

Courtesy of Mammoth Mountain

D ave McCoy's first ski competition was not quite as successful as he would have hoped. At the dares of several Norwegian mining friends, he fashioned a pair of homemade boards and appeared at the Class B Jump at Snoqualmie Pass in Washington. Not surprisingly, he didn't just fall, his jump landed him ingloriously in Snoqualmie Creek. But the waters of that high alpine creek couldn't douse McCoy's competitive fire. He went on to become California State Champion in 1941.

It took McCoy four years to recover from the leg-shattering accident that ended his own racing career in 1942. Once on skis again, he began working with kids, and by 1949 he had his first junior champion, Charlotte Zumstein.

When McCoy's portable rope tows had to be moved, local kids helped him set up the tows and got to ski for free. He would coach them whenever he could. "I liked doing it; I just like kids." The young skiers were always expected to work by picking up trash, washing dishes or busing tables in the lodge cafeteria as part of their ski training. "We'd get up at three o'clock in the morning and climb the mountain, ski for half a day and then they'd help me work."

McCoy's experience taught him that each skier was an individual. He became more than a coach to his youngsters and they called him "Pa." He led by example and a lot of hard skiing. "They didn't all do the same thing. The physical aspect of it was different for each one, because they had different physical capabilities. Their mental approach to things was different. Their reason for doing it was different, so you kept that in mind. Some kids you would work with seven days a week, and some days you'd just put everything else aside to do things for them. Some are still here today, fifty years old or so. Isn't that something?"

One of his prize pupils, Jill Kinmont, in 1955 became the only female ever to win both the junior and senior women's slalom title. Her brother Bob won the Men's Senior Nationals the same year. Jean Saubert, racing in the 1964 Innsbruck

Jean Saubert, one of McCoy's winning women skiers. She won two medals in the 1964 Innsbruck Winter Olympic Games.

Courtesy of Alpine Meadows

Charlotte Zumstein, Dave's first junior champion.

Courtesy of Carson White

Winter Olympic Games, won two medals. At the 1965 U.S. Nationals, Mammoth women placed first, second, fourth, sixth and seventh in the downhill, first through fourth in slalom and first through fourth in the combined.

The next year, 1966, the American women's F.I.S. Team at the World Championships in Chile was comprised completely of Mammoth racers, including McCoy's daughter Penny who captured the bronze medal in slalom. Cathy Allen took fifth place, and her sister Wendy won the Sun Valley Challenge Cup, the first American woman to win an international race all season.

Three of McCoy's other children, Gary, Dennis "Poncho" and Carl, also became top-level racers. In 1966, Mammoth Mountain put fourteen kids on the U.S. Ski Team.

"The whole school was let out so the kids could help us pull the cables in. To me, the time I spent coaching those kids was when I developed my management skills. They gave me that."

Courtesy of Mammoth Mountain

The Mammoth Race Team at the Sun Valley races in 1952. Dave is kneeling, and Jill Kinmont is on the far right.

He influenced his racers beyond the race course. His motto, "Be smart, be alert and be aware. When you have all those things working for you, you look at life almost the same way. There's no person with excitement and enthusiasm that doesn't learn and progress and isn't on top in whatever his endeavors are." McCoy never had a formula for coaching. "We just skied," says Jill Kinmont, "usually just trying to keep up with Dave."

1915 – 1995

"In the early days, he would venture far and wide with his dog Penny, his friends Marty, Bill and Barney, exploring every nook, fishing every brook and skiing every slope. From the beginning he had a strong desire to share his passions and simple pleasures with those around him," says son, Craig Poulsen.

"Y ou're going to live in Squaw Valley," Wayne Poulsen told his future wife, Gladys "Sandy" Kunau, shortly after meeting her on the ski slopes of Idaho in 1941. "'That's interesting', I told him," she recalls. "Of course, he hadn't even started buying any property, and I had no idea what he was talking about. Nobody had even heard of Squaw Valley."

Poulsen, born and raised in Reno, Nevada, knew Squaw Valley and had planned on living there for a long time. He had first visited the valley in the early 30s on a fishing trip with his best friend Marty Arrougé whose father had at one time been a sheepherder in Squaw's meadow.

The mountains and the outdoors were Poulsen's proving grounds. When he was ten, he made his first pair of skis fashioned from seven-foot slats of Oregon pine, the tips softened and shaped after soaking them in a nearby hot spring.

"I met Dr. James Church (known as the 'father of modern snow surveying') when I was twelve years old," said Poulsen in an interview several years ago. "By the time I was sixteen, I was a good enough skier to go on his snow surveys. I used to climb Mount Rose once a week. In 1937 I spent practically the whole winter on top, determining water capacity, surveying and calculating how much water would be in the Truckee River."

Poulsen and Arrougé returned to Squaw Valley to fish and hike whenever they could. The more he saw of it, the more Poulsen liked the protected valley surrounded by granite peaks. "Wayne and I thought about the valley and what we could do," remembers Arrougé. "We were dreamers. We'd look up at those slopes and say to each other, what a schuss that would be!"

In the wintertime Poulsen and Arrougé began climbing the area's highest crags and furthermost bowls. They discovered multiple fall lines, from soft rolling shoulders to spirited steeps. "Wayne really liked the area and wanted to develop it as a ski resort. He began talking to various people about the possibility of buying it up," says Arrougé.

Ski jumping was the major discipline at the time, and Poulsen was becoming one of the best, competing with the top guns of the era, including Olympian Roy Mikkelsen. The confident young skier became part of a barnstorming group that created ski jumping exhibitions at unlikely sites such as the Los Angeles Coliseum, the Oakland Auditorium and the 1939 San Francisco World's Fair at Treasure Island.

At a jump constructed on the University of California, Berkeley campus, Poulsen once transported six carloads of snow from Cisco Grove to jump in front of an estimated crowd of 50,000. An article that appeared in the *San Francisco Examiner* reported on one of his exhibitions in 1933: "All season long Poulsen has been landing the full weight of his body on a badly sprained ankle. At the Expo, when the Utah boys failed to show and the audience had to have some more jumping, Wayne sprained his ankle on his first jump, taped it up and repeated four times, only to break his leg on the last attempt."

© Carolyn Caddes

Wayne and Sandy Poulsen were married for fifty-three years and raised eight children,
four of whom raced on the U.S. Ski Team.

Wayne Poulsen on his Mount Rose Upski tow.

Courtesy of Sandy Poulsen

That year, Poulsen organized the first ski team at the University of Nevada, Reno. He became California State Champion in downhill, slalom, jumping and langlauf and led his team to three Pacific Coast Intercollegiate Championships. After his graduation from the university in 1938, Poulsen opened Mount Rose Upski, Nevada's first ski area.

"It was the end of the Depression, and jobs were scarce," said Poulsen. "I didn't have a job so I made one up for me—owner of a ski area. We offered a gasoline-operated rope tow that took skiers 560 feet to the top. I ran the ski school, and a warming hut offered a pot-bellied stove, hot lunch, drinks and ski rentals. We even had a slot machine that eventually broke down. A mouse somehow got into it, but it looked good sitting inside."

After three years, Poulsen's renewal on his lease was blocked by the ski area's landowner who, impressed with the resort's success, decided to run things himself. It was a harsh setback, yet in a homespun philosophy that would mark his character throughout his life, Poulsen remembers thinking, "The war had begun, and everything else seemed pretty trivial."

Urged by Arrougé who had become a flight instructor for the U.S. Army Air Corps, Poulsen entered flight training. Thus began an impressive military career that spanned three wars. While on leave in 1942, he wed Sandy. The following year he purchased 640 acres in Squaw Valley from Southern Pacific, and continued to eye it as a ski operation.

"From the beginning we had the idea for Squaw as a destination resort," says Sandy. During winter months they'd often leave their car parked on the main road and ski in, wading through Squaw's icy creek and climbing the mountain on skins. "After the war Wayne brought in friends, some Olympic-caliber skiers such as André Roch and Friedl Pfeifer, to help advise on the best runs and the best snow. Each time we would approach the mountain from a different angle."

"One day we decided to climb to the top of one of the peaks. I remember standing at the top and watching all seven other skiers create mini avalanches as they skied to the valley floor. I said to myself, 'I can't do this. I'm going to be here until spring.' Wayne was always telling me that I was a better skier than I thought. However, that hill was too steep. So I carefully skied from tree group to tree group, making my kick turns out of sight, I thought. When I reached the bottom, Wayne said to me, 'That was twenty-two kick turns I counted. I'll think I'll name this run KT-22.'"

Sandy and Wayne at Sugar Bowl before they were married.

Courtesy of Sandy Poulsen

Poulsen's military flight experience earned him a job with Pan American Airlines. Soon he was establishing the first flights across the Pacific to Asia, as well as the historic maiden voyage over the North Pole from San Francisco to Paris. Although the Pan Am job supported Poulsen's growing family, money for a ski resort remained in short supply.

In need of financing, the Poulsens began introducing friends and potential investors to their valley for a day of skiing. Eventually, they purchased a World War II amphibious vehicle called a Weasel, which they named the "Clipper Reindeer" in honor of Poulsen's Pan Am affiliation, to shuttle skiers across the valley floor to the base of Squaw Peak.

"People would be skijoring behind the Weasel. We built a primitive bridge so everybody wouldn't have to take their clothes off to cross the creek. I'd make a big pot of chili. We had interest from many people, including Corty Hill, an enormously wealthy person who had helped develop Sugar Bowl," says Sandy.

It was during this period that the Poulsens brought Alex Cushing to Squaw Valley as a potential investor. By the spring of 1948, Poulsen and Cushing had formed the Squaw Valley Development Corporation, with Poulsen serving as its first president and Cushing as secretary-treasurer. From the beginning their partnership was marred by conflict and dispute.

Skijoring in Squaw Valley behind the Clipper Reindeer. Alex Cushing is the fourth from the right behind waving Carson White in shorts and Vi White in her signature straw hat.

A bitter disagreement broke up the partnership shortly before Squaw Valley's opening on Thanksgiving Day 1949, but Poulsen didn't consider leaving his beloved valley. "Wayne had no hate in him at all. He was a very strong person. He didn't allow what happened to spoil his life," recalls Sandy.

Poulsen never earned a dime directly off the ski operation, but he had the foresight to purchase the rest of the land within the valley, close to 2,000 acres. He also took on the enormous job of developing the Squaw Valley community, building the roads and other amenities to access the lots that began selling for $750.

Poulsen started his own ski operation, called Papoose, on land he owned in the valley. There he built a ski jump and coached local children. Beginning in 1967, each Easter he held a slalom event at Papoose for young racers. Their names are on a perpetual trophy that still rests in the Poulsen home, and many who participated became members of the U.S. Olympic and National teams.

My father did suffer many setbacks,"
says son, Craig Poulsen,
"but the essence of his dreams was never compromised.
He always dealt with setbacks in his own philosophical manner.
He knew in his heart what really mattered—
his passions, his family and his friends."

Possibly his greatest accomplishment occurred prior to the 1960 Winter Olympic Games when Poulsen, acting alone, harassed county and state officials to a standstill over the possible ruin of 150 acres of Squaw Valley meadow.

"They wanted to put a sewage treatment plant, actually an open sludge bed, at the east end of the meadow," recalls Craig. "They wanted to pave fifty acres of meadow, gravel fifty and lay compacted sawdust over another fifty. Back then, there were no environmental funds or agencies. My father fought those officials all by himself and out of his own pocket. He saved the meadow from total destruction."

"Wayne Poulsen in the last years of his life remained a quiet, intelligent man with a warm sense of humor," says Craig of his father. "You would often hear him say, 'It doesn't matter, besides the fish are rising and the skiing is fine. Come on boys, it's time to go!'"

In 1980 Poulsen was elected to the U.S. National Ski Hall of Fame. Soon after, he contracted a debilitating form of Parkinson's disease and died in 1995. The California Trade and Commerce Agency posthumously inducted Poulsen into the California Tourism Hall of Fame where his name joins others of equal stature: Walt Disney, Howard Hughes, Ansel Adams and William Randolph Hearst.

The Poulsen family in the Squaw Valley meadow near their home.

Above Squaw Valley.

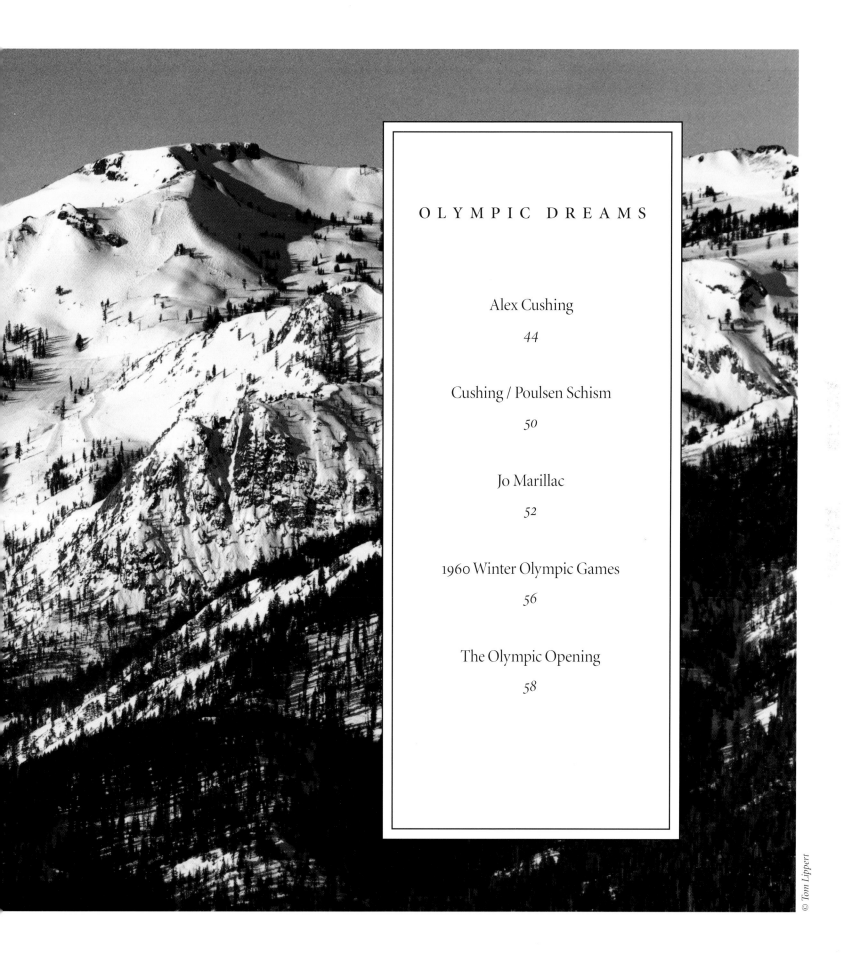

OLYMPIC DREAMS

*"Nothing is smooth sailing
if it's going to be any good.
Squaw Valley is for
everyone to see.
It's been a remarkable
fifty years, but I'm looking to
the future, to do what
I think should be done here.
The changes that are going
to take place are like nothing
anybody has dreamed of.
I'm just trying to stay alive
to see them."*

lex Cushing admits he was probably the least-suited person to become a ski area operator, "I have an affinity to the sea more than the mountains." Yet, his vision has made Squaw Valley one of the world's best-known resorts.

Cushing's first time on skis was a failure. Escorting a debutante to her train leaving New York for Montréal on a ski vacation, the tuxedo-clad, intoxicated nineteen-year-old piled onto the train and never got off. Two days later, wearing his tuxedo pants, he put on a pair of skis and entered a race.

"The owner of the resort, known as 'The Marquis,' couldn't stand me. I had crashed at the finish line, and the skis had just exploded into toothpicks. The Marquis came over, disgusted, and said 'Cushing, you are disqualified!' He became even more irate when he discovered it was his skis that I'd borrowed."

The unruly redhead stubbornly continued to ski, but admits that he struggled for years, forever stepping out of his bindings and losing skis on the easiest of slopes.

Born in 1913, the grandson of a wealthy Boston tea merchant, Cushing was educated at Groton and Harvard. He graduated from Harvard Law School and practiced law until World War II, when he enlisted in the Navy. As a troubleshooter and Lieut. Commander for the Naval Air Transport Service, he was in charge of securing dockage equipment for the military during the war. It was a frustrating and exhausting undertaking, and Cushing paid the price for his efforts. Collapsing after working without sleep for sixty hours, he awoke in Bethesda Naval Hospital with his face completely paralyzed. A partial paralysis on the left side of his face remains, so that Cushing appears to sport a perpetual scowl no matter what his mood. After the war, he was hired by a law firm in New York.

However, it was a ski vacation to Alta, Utah, and a chance meeting with Wayne Poulsen that altered the course of the bright, young man's life. "I asked him where the best skiing was. He answered, the best skiing in America was a place in California where he owned land."

Impulsively, Cushing traveled to the Sierra Nevada with his best friend Alexander McFadden in 1946. They hiked in from the highway with Poulsen to view Squaw Valley's immense amphitheater. "McFadden commented to me that you could fit a couple of Sun Valleys in it. Two years later Poulsen and I formed the Squaw Valley Development Corporation."

It was a decision that was easy to make. "I wanted a change. I had to get out of the city. Frankly, I would have never embarked in the ski business if it hadn't been for my wartime experiences. The war taught me how interesting life could be, that there were far more possibilities than sitting in a law office on Wall Street."

Educated, privileged and comfortable with the upperclass, Cushing knew that inexperience was not a barrier to realizing his dream. "I was very unqualified to operate a ski area. I was the wise guy from the East. However, I was able to raise $400,000. My wife Justine and I scraped together

© Carolyn Caddes

"Our goal is to be the best ski resort in the country,"
the patriarch of one of North America's controversial yet greatest resorts says.
When asked to play a certain song, he replied, "I only play in the key of C."

$125,000, every personal cent we had, and we persuaded other friends to invest, including Lawrence Rockefeller."

Squaw Valley opened to the public on Thanksgiving Day 1949 with a small lodge, a rope tow, and a ski lift built by Heron Engineering, billed as the longest double chairlift in the world. Revolutionary in design and operation, it became Squaw's key to business. However, to Cushing the future wasn't certain. "We were broke the day we opened. We were way under-capitalized. The total revenues from the first year were $28,000."

Besides monetary problems and sharp differences with Poulsen that eventually led to the dissolution of their partnership, Cushing dealt with the roar of Sierra Nevada storms. In Squaw's first five years of operation, avalanches ripped out lift towers three times. The lodge was cut off four times by bridge washouts and twice flooded.

"During the big winter of 1952, our lift went down and it took six weeks to repair. It should have killed us as a business." Fortunately, the roads were closed at the same time, and the company's business insurance paid Cushing $1,000 a day, allowing time and money to fix the lift. By the time the roads were open, Squaw Valley was back in operation.

One day in 1954, a two-paragraph story in the *San Francisco Chronicle* caught Cushing's eye. Reno had bid for the 1960 Winter Olympic Games. A brainstorm swept over him like an avalanche. Why not get Squaw Valley some free press by applying for the Games? *Time* magazine later quoted Cushing in a 1959 interview: "I had no more interest in getting the Olympics than the man on the moon."

It began as an advertising gimmick and turned into a wild dream. In fact, all that Squaw could offer was one ski lift, two rope tows, a small ski lodge, magnificent terrain and promises. Yet Cushing was not one to be deterred.

Calling the U.S. Olympic headquarters in New York, Cushing discovered that he would have to make a formal presentation at the next meeting only a month away. He immediately enlisted the support of then California Governor Goodwin Knight, as well as two state senators. Reviving an old bill that had promised money for the Los Angeles Olympic Games in 1932, California legislators passed a new version appropriating $1 million. With guaranteed financial backing, a smooth-talking Cushing made his presentation to the U.S. Olympic group.

"When I'm convinced of something, I can be a very persuasive speaker." His address worked, humbling shocked representatives from the more established ski areas nominated: Lake Placid, Sun Valley and Aspen. "If you ask me," responded one disgruntled rival, "Squaw Valley is a figment of Cushing's imagination." Figment or not, the promotion-minded Cushing had pushed his resort beyond anyone's expectations. Squaw Valley became the American nominee before the International Olympic Committee.

"You don't want to be in something where the other guy likes it better than you do. You can't compete with them. On the other hand, if you get into something that you like, then you don't know when you're working and when you're not. The ski business, though hard work, has always been that to me."

"Once nominated, I said 'What do we do now?' I was told to visit Avery Brundage, president of the International Olympic Committee." Cushing recalls the meeting with the protocol-minded Brundage in his Chicago office. "Without looking up from his desk, Brundage said to me, 'The U.S. Olympic Committee obviously has taken leave of their senses.' He told me that there's no chance they'll accept Squaw Valley, that I had no idea what I was up against. He then told me I had set the Olympic movement back twenty-five years."

Eventually, Brundage and Cushing became friends. "I even called him 'Daddy.' Of course, after we were voted the Games, he told me that the reason I won was because they wanted to pay him a delicate compliment as head of the I.O.C. He always had to let you know who was boss."

The success of the Squaw Valley Olympics created a surge of development in the Tahoe Basin. While growth and money flowed into nearby Lake Tahoe, Squaw Valley, surprisingly, didn't capitalize on its international acclaim. Despite the resort's prestige as the largest Tahoe ski area, Squaw Valley fell steadily into disrepair.

"I had one hand tied behind my back. The Olympic Games enjoyed a great success, but then came a ten-year stint of trying to get rid of those Games. Dealing with state and federal politics was a terrible situation. It was chaos. That's when Squaw got a bad reputation. The state's the one who altered the stream and the meadow and made things different. We had to overcome the environmental degradation the state did."

Cushing says that part of the problem existed because he lived in two different places, spending most of his time in New York and Newport. "My wife was a marvelous woman, but she enjoyed back East more than out here." He also had a penchant for being obstinate and arrogant with regulatory agencies, sometimes ignoring the rules while pushing ahead with projects without proper permits or planning.

"In those early days I could really bait officials. It was very stupid on my part. I'd practically say, come and get me. Of course, you can't do that today. They *will* come and get you." Cushing admits that when the ski area was struggling, he made plenty of mistakes. "I just did it. It was the only way to get something like this built. I couldn't afford to screw around. They wouldn't let me cut down some trees on KT-22. I told them of the liability they presented. Two people ended up hitting those trees and dying. I took them out. I won't apologize for anything I did."

Seven serious chairlift accidents resulting in serious injury would hinder the resort's reputation during the 1960s, but no tragedy would come close to the aerial cable car accident on April 15, 1978. During a freak spring storm, one of the cables dislodged from its track, piercing the roof of the cable car and crushing four skiers to death inside.

Courtesy of Robert Frohlich

The first gondola at Squaw Valley.

"I felt a personal responsibility for all those people. Squaw Valley's problems had to be addressed and sorted out. There comes a period in your life when you start thinking, 'Is this the best I can do?' No, it wasn't."

Cushing committed himself to improving Squaw Valley and became a more permanent fixture at the resort. First, he repaired and upgraded the aerial cable car. Then, he invested millions in an extensive overhaul of the base lodge and a complete refurbishment of Gold Coast at the top of Squaw's gondola. In 1985 Squaw Valley installed the first of several state-of-the-art, high-speed, detachable quad chairlifts.

In the late 1980s Cushing married Nancy Wente, now president of Squaw Valley Ski Corporation. With her help, Squaw Valley's development exploded into activity. In 1989 Squaw Valley began a $15 million renovation at High Camp, the top terminal of the aerial cable car. Calling it an "eighth wonder of the world," and his happiest achievement, the project included an Olympic-size, open-air ice rink; restaurants; tennis courts; a bungee-jumping complex; and a swimming lagoon.

Emile Allais and Alex Cushing confer during the 1969 World Cup at Squaw Valley.

Courtesy of Robert Frohlich

What started as a tiny tempest in a remote Sierra teapot in 1949, once described by an Olympic official as a "low-class picnic area," bloomed into a great and glittering resort during the 1990s.

Not content with close to fifty years of remarkable history, Cushing continues to push his resort toward brave new worlds. He has announced a master plan for an alpine village spread over what is now Squaw Valley's 20-acre parking lot to be built by Intrawest, a Canadian investment group.

In early 1997 Cushing unveiled a $30 million project calling for the installation of the Funitel, a high-speed tram system, resistent to high winds, and the High Camp Pulse, a non-detachable conveyance connecting the upper mountain station Gold Coast to High Camp. Three hotels, to be started before the turn of the century, are planned for the upper mountain. "We're pushing ahead into the 21st century. We're proud of our Olympic heritage, but we look forward to an even greater future."

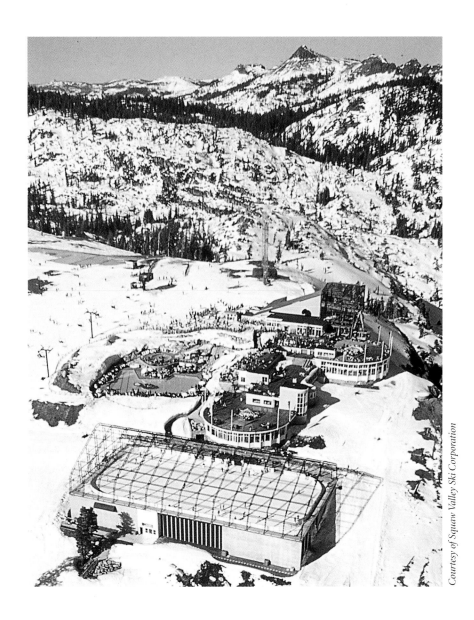

Courtesy of Squaw Valley Ski Corporation

"Like Courchevel in Europe,
this has been a concept of mine
to have two elevations,
6,200 feet and 8,200 feet,
that offer something to visitors.
It may be a pie in the sky
to some, but we're fixing up
things below, too.
People forget that I'm in the
uphill transportation business.
We still have to earn our money,
and High Camp is designed
to sell car rides."

In the spring of 1948, Wayne Poulsen and Alex Cushing formed the Squaw Valley Development Corporation and pooled their resources. Poulsen supplied 640 acres, and Cushing $400,000. Alex and his first wife, Justine, invested $125,000 of their own money, "every personal cent we had." Their former school chum, Lawrence Rockefeller, put up $50,000, and the remaining investment came from other friends. Poulsen traded his land for company stock.

"Wayne's big mistake was not leasing his land to the company, even if only for one percent per year," says his wife Sandy Poulsen. "That way he'd have always maintained ownership. Instead, he eventually lost his land by trading it to the corporation for stock. I guess he was pretty naive, but that was Wayne. He trusted everybody."

Even before the resort's Thanksgiving Day opening in 1949 when around 100 skiers paid four dollars each to ride the world's first double chairlift, Poulsen and Cushing had sharp differences which eventually dissolved their friendship and business relationship.

"Wayne and I had differences in the very beginning of the company," admits Cushing. "He wanted the company to be in the lift and land business. In fact, he told me we could buy the whole valley for $50,000. But the last thing I wanted to do was to go into real estate, a business I don't understand. I wanted to be in the uphill transportation business, and I raised the money on that basis."

Cushing wanted to operate a bar, restaurant and hotel, while Poulsen felt those facilities should be leased out. There was a dispute about the dispersion of Poulsen's land holding to the company. Forty-two acres of land had been reserved by Poulsen as homesites; that left the resort with only six acres of level ground.

Photo by John Corbett. Courtesy of Carson White

Squaw Valley before there were lifts.

Increasingly irked by Poulsen's absences as a Pan Am international pilot, Cushing went ahead and bought a set of surplus Air Force barracks, had them trucked into the valley and put the corporation in the hotel business.

Cushing and Sandy Poulsen no longer comment on exactly what transpired, but according to a February 1959 *Time* magazine article, the showdown came about in October 1949 when Cushing called a stockholders' meeting while Poulsen was away flying for Pan Am. The result was inevitable, since Cushing owned 52% of the stock and his friends another 46%. After an audit showed nothing legally wrong, Cushing, who was secretary-treasurer of the company, replaced Poulsen as president of Squaw Valley Development Corporation. Since only one lift permit was allotted to the area by the U.S. Forest Service, Cushing retained exclusive rights for ski operations.

Poulsen still owned a majority of the valley floor, but he had effectively lost control of the ski operations, and would never make a dime directly off the resort.

While Poulsen would do very well in his real estate business, his dream for Squaw Valley was lost, and he and Cushing would remain adversaries to the end. "We sold all the stockholders on the idea of the lift business," Poulsen said in a 1988 interview. "The hotel business did not turn out well. The hotel and ski business just didn't mix."

Cushing is reluctant to talk about the ill-fated partnership that founded one of the world's greatest ski areas. "I don't think there's anything to be gained by it. Our animosities hurt the valley. By and large it doesn't exist anymore. Wayne has gone on to his reward. Everybody is working for the benefit of the valley."

© *Ray Atkeson*

JO MARILLAC

SQUAW VALLEY

"In 1954 Alex Cushing came to me and said, 'I'm going to ask you a question, and you must answer it simply yes or no.' He asked me if I thought Squaw Valley could put on the Olympics. I answered 'yes because of the mountain, but no because of the facilities.' The yes part was all that Cushing needed."

J o Marillac, born in the small French village of Ancelle in the Dauphine Alps in 1921, tells his tale in a thickly preserved accent. "Mr. Cushing had read that Reno and Sun Valley applied for the Olympics. He told me, 'They're getting all this free publicity!' He wanted to jump on the same bandwagon."

Marillac chuckles. Even his chuckle sounds French, and he scratches a small scar beneath his left eye, the one he received from a bike-racing crash as a youth. He remembers his arrival in Squaw Valley in 1953 at the invitation of his friend and the resort's first ski school director, French skiing luminary Emile Allais. "Emile drove me up from San Francisco. It was only fall, but there was four feet of snow along the roadside. Emile told me this was nothing. The real snow was higher up."

Along with a handful of other expert skiers, like Pascal Heuga, Dodie Post, Stan Tomlinson and Dick Reuter, who had moved to the small alpine community, Marillac discovered skiing that bordered on the divine. "Mon Dieu! There was so much snow! I love deep powder and we were able to ski deep, untracked snow every run, all day after storms. I couldn't believe it. I was very impressed."

When Alex Cushing applied to the U.S. Olympic Committee, the obscure resort had one chair lift, two rope tows and a small day lodge. "Great grief, Alex," gasped Donna Fox of the U.S. Olympic Committee when she first read Cushing's proposal, "you have nothing but a glorified picnic ground." He may have had little more than a wild dream, but he also held a trump card few others could have foreseen: Jo Marillac.

Still respected as a war hero with the French Resistance and the youngest mountaineer ever to be fully certified as a "High Mountain Guide" in the French Alps, Marillac used his contacts with the French government to win the support of the International Federation of Skiing (F.I.S.) and the International Olympic Committee (I.O.C.) delegates. "We traveled six weeks throughout Europe. The hardest part was not convincing the delegates that we could build the necessary facilities, since Europeans believed strongly in American construction—to them, Americans could build things quicker and better than anyone in the world—it was more if Squaw Valley had a mountain equal to the other great European resorts bidding for the Games."

To aid in the sales effort, Cushing also hired two fellow Harvard classmates, George Weller, a globe-trotting reporter for the Chicago *Daily News,* and Marshall Haseltine, an urbane expatriate who lived in Europe. While Weller toured South America and Scandinavia to pitch the Olympics, Cushing, Marillac and Haseltine lobbied European I.O.C. representatives. Cushing even spent $3,000 on a 12-by-6-foot model of Squaw Valley that he presented to delegates in Paris.

Despite all the preparation, European resistance was severe. Huffed a German delegate to Cushing at one point, "Don't think you are going to parlay one ski lift into an Olympic Games." Cushing, who had made enemies within his country's own Olympic committee because of his Cinderella win over more famed resorts such as Sun Valley, Aspen and Lake Placid, had a U.S. delegate threaten, "Who's going to vote for you? I'm not."

© *Carolyn Caddes*

"If you want to live in the mountains, this is where you'd like to make your place.
You cannot build a mountain. Squaw has an incredible mixture and blend of terrain for the expert to beginner.
I've been very fortunate to make my life here. Olympics or not, these are tremendous mountains."

It was then that Jo Marillac, known for his word and integrity, proved invaluable. "Many delegates came to me. They said, 'You know the ski resorts. We don't know Squaw Valley. We believe you. You explain to us.'" The international delegates asked him to compare Squaw Valley to a ski resort in Europe. "I said Kitzbühel. It's the only ski resort like Squaw Valley that you ski from the very top of the mountain to the bottom." Marillac assured them of Squaw's reliable snow conditions. He pointed out that six of the last seven Winter Olympic Games had been in Europe. Now it was the United States' chance. "They kept saying, we don't have this or that, that Squaw Valley can't have an Olympics. I told them, 'I'm here to tell you we can.'"

Those were convincing words from a man who had avoided a Nazi firing squad by escaping from an impregnable prison four times; who set a record climbing one of Europe's tallest peaks—five and a half hours on the precipitous north face of the Aiguille des Drus; and who was awarded the Medaille d'Argent in 1950 as France's greatest all-around athlete.

Acting on Marillac's judgment, the F.I.S. backed Squaw, and at a crucial meeting in Paris in June 1955, the Tahoe resort won its bid, 32–30, over Innsbruck on the second ballot. Squaw Valley had achieved the impossible.

And while it was Marillac who played a large role in bringing the Olympics to Squaw Valley, he found himself on the outside looking in during the course of the Games. "I remember the day of the hockey game between the Russians and Americans. I was walking in the parking lot, and Mr. Sakata from the Japanese Olympic Committee saw me and asked why wasn't I at the hockey game?" Marillac, whose duties were terminated after the vote in Europe, was not asked to participate during the Olympics, even as a host. He had neither ticket nor credentials. "Mr. Sakata says 'What? You were the person to get these Olympics! No ticket? Come with me.'" For the rest of the Olympics, Jo Marillac was credentialed as an official member of the Japanese delegation.

"I was very glad Squaw Valley had the Olympics. I always told them we could have the Olympics. You go to Europe today and people stop you if you say you live in Squaw Valley. The Olympics made the resort very famous."

Jo Marillac with Jean-Claude Killy and other French racers at Squaw Valley.

Courtesy of Jo Marillac

After seventeen years as Squaw Valley Ski School director, Marillac moved on to a successful real estate career. He retired in the mid-80s and still lives in the home he built in 1953. To a mountaineer, home is where you hang your ice axe. Marillac's axe, scarred from combat with many mountains, hangs on the wall of his living room overlooking Squaw Valley meadow.

© Ray Atkeson

Jo Marillac plunging down Headwall in 1961. Lake Tahoe can be seen in the background under the clouds.

The 1960 Squaw Valley Winter Olympic Games included twenty-seven events and 700 athletes. A daily ticket cost $7.50 and allowed a spectator to see at least five major events. It was also the first time the Games were televised daily. CBS had paid $50,000 for broadcasting rights, and Walter Cronkite was the host.

New events that year included women's speed skating and the biathlon. In another innovation, scoring and other information was computed electronically and transmitted directly to scoreboards.

The Japanese ski jumping team competed for the first time, and its members became favorites with the crowd because of their revolutionary jumping technique. While other jumpers kept their arms outstretched for balance, the Japanese held their arms to their sides for better aerodynamics. Jean Vuarnet, a lightly regarded member of the French Team, startled the ski world by winning the gold in downhill. Using metal skis for the first time in international competition and developing an egg position tuck, he carried the French to a surprise victory.

The United States went on to win three gold, four silver and two bronze medals. The American medalists included speed skaters Bill Disney and Jeanne Ashworth, figure skaters Carol Heiss, Barbara Ann Roles and David Jenkins, and skiers Betsy Snite and Penny Pitou.

While the gold eluded Pitou, a team of young American hockey players was stealing hearts as it skated to one dramatic victory after another. Before the Games the U.S. hockey squad hardly seemed a team of destiny in losing to Denver University and Michigan Tech in pre-Olympic play. However, at Squaw Valley the Americans solidly defeated Sweden and West Germany before facing a favored Canadian team. The Americans won 2–1 as goalie Jack McCartan turned back a barrage of shots in the second period, making 38 saves in all.

The Americans met the defending champion Soviet team two days later in a stirring contest much like the one played at

Penny Pitou gave reporters a candid view of her goals at Squaw. "If someone asked me if I wanted a 300SL Mercedes or a six-year college scholarship, I wouldn't want either. The Olympics are the only thing I want." Here she is waiting for the results of the race that would bring her one of two silver medals.

Courtesy of Craig Beck

Action on the speed skating oval.

Courtesy of Craig Beck

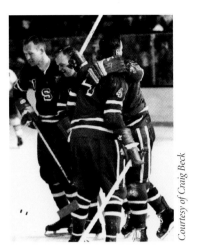

In the final game, an exhausted and tense U.S. team trailed Czechoslovakia after two periods, 4–3. During the final break, Nikolai Sologubov, the Soviet captain, visited the Americans' dressing room and advised them to take oxygen. A tank was found, and the revived American team went on a rampage, scoring six goals to win 9–4 and secure the gold medal.

Lake Placid twenty years later. Watched by the spectators jamming Blythe Arena and a national television audience, the Americans were down 2–1 before tying the game and going ahead with five minutes remaining. McCartan protected the net, and for the first time, the U.S. had beaten the Soviets in hockey.

By nearly any accounting, the Squaw Valley Olympics was a successful show. It attracted an estimated 240,000 spectators and a cavalcade of attention to a remote and once inaccessible mountain hollow in the Sierra Nevada.

"The Squaw Valley Olympics are what I consider to be the last great Olympics," says Jimmie Heuga, who was not a competitor in 1960, but won a bronze medal in the slalom at Innsbruck in 1964. "All the events except cross-country were within walking distance of each other, giving the Games an intimacy absent since. Those Olympics reminded you of what the Games were supposed to be about. The athletes were able to meet each other. You'd see Russian skaters walking with Italian speed skaters. Athletes were able to watch other events besides their own."

Carol Heiss executing the compulsory school figures, a sight no longer seen in figure skating competitions.

The entrance to the 1960 Olympic Winter Games at Squaw Valley with Blythe Arena, the skating oval and jumping hill.

OPENING THE 1960 WINTER OLYMPIC GAMES

Two months before the Games were to begin, warm weather and lack of snow so alarmed event organizers that Native Americans from a Paiute tribe were brought in to dispel the thaw with a ceremonial dance. Then two weeks before the opening ceremonies, a storm brought torrential rains and winds up to 100 miles per hour, followed by a blizzard that would not stop. Andrea Mead Lawrence, who was to ski down Red Dog with the Olympic flame, had gone out the day before for her rehearsal with the National Ski Patrol. The storm continued through the night. By morning, new snow had drifted over the back side of icy bumps. The parade of nations began behind a curtain of snow, setting the stage for the countless millions watching on television.

"Without the aid of poles, I was to ski down the steep face of Red Dog carrying the torch high above my head. I was really worried about losing it and falling in front of the world. Right up to the moment of skiing the torch down, it was still storming. I remember they had a tough time lighting the torch. At the countdown, the weather turned beautiful. I came down. The honor guard skied behind me nicely controlled. There was a huge crowd and everybody was cheering."

Courtesy of Craig Beck

"It was an astonishing moment." Andrea Mead Lawrence remembers of her experience skiing with the Olympic Torch from the top of Red Dog Peak into Blythe Arena to commence the 1960 Winter Olympic Games in Squaw Valley. *"It remains a wonderful moment in my life. My Olympic memories have clearly influenced how I think and live. The Olympic spirit is special and inspiring. The Squaw Valley Olympics really captured those Olympic ideals. I was just happy to be a part of it."*

Above Kirkwood.

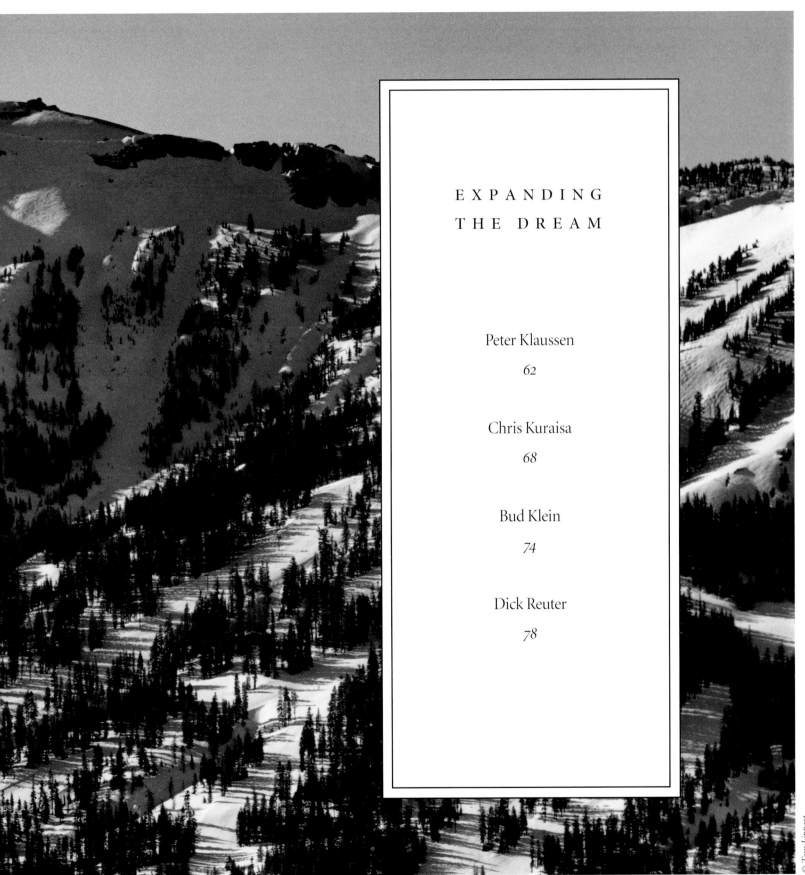

EXPANDING THE DREAM

© *Tom Lippert*

P E T E R

K L A U S S E N

—

A L P I N E

M E A D O W S

*"I insisted we build our first lift
all the way to the top.
It was conceived as a
family resort to be built by
skiers for skiers."*

hen Peter Klaussen first visited the Sierra Nevada in 1955, you could buy frontage property on Lake Tahoe's North Shore for $10,000, or a buildable homesite in Squaw Valley for $2,500. You could build a ski resort at a start-up cost of $750,000.

"It doesn't seem like much in today's ski world, especially when you consider modern mountain homes that cost a lot more, but for John Reily, who began the project, it turned out to be too much money." In a slow, thoughtful pace, Peter Klaussen tells the story of Alpine Meadows' conception and his tenure there as its first general manager.

In the mid-50s, Reily, treasurer of the Carnation Company and chairman of the Los Angeles Chamber of Commerce, built a cabin in Squaw Valley. Two years later he acquired land at the top of Squaw Valley's KT-22 lift from Southern Pacific and built, with Klaussen's help, a day lodge and restaurant called the "Cornice." From this vantage point, Reily saw the potential for a new ski area.

"John was full of ideas. He wanted an alternative to Squaw Valley, something more relaxed and comfortable for families. Originally, he just wanted a little resort that would have summer access by a jeep road. In winter he'd run a lift up the backside of Red Dog. People could come in on snow vehicles and ski the backside of KT. John also had a notion of building a gondola from KT to the top of Ward Peak, something he thought would be quite spectacular, but he would have had to depend on Squaw Valley access for people to ride it."

An Amherst College and Harvard Business School graduate, Klaussen had quit his corporate job with Polaroid and moved to Squaw Valley in 1955 because of his love of the mountains. While schooled in business, he was an avid skier with a keen sense of design and terrain.

It was during the planning stages of the 1960 Squaw Valley Olympics, and later while helping control the avalanche hazards during the Games, that Klaussen discovered the perfect ski area. He had skied into Bear Creek Valley with Willi Schaeffler and Nelson Bennett, two technical directors for the Olympics searching for a biathlon course, when he saw four distinct bowls descending from the crest, all with different terrain. The land between the valley and bowls was so sparse of fir and pine that little clearing would be necessary.

"I told John that the terrain where he was thinking about for his ski area was all wrong. The exposure was southern. The sun would melt the snow. It's too steep and windy on that side of KT, but I told him there was a possibility for a grand resort next to Squaw Peak."

At Klaussen's urging, Reily applied for and was granted a permit from the U.S. Forest Service. He then persuaded others to become involved: C. Minot Dole, founder of the National Ski Patrol; Robert P. McCulloch of McCulloch chain saws; William Kimball, former president of the Sierra Club; and George Hart, director of the First National Bank and Liberty Mutual Insurance Company. They enthusiastically joined with him to form a corporation.

© Carolyn Caddes

In six months, from July to December 1961, Peter Klaussen,
in charge of construction for Alpine Meadows,
created a ski resort from scratch.

The group offered 140,000 shares of common stock at $10 a share in a plan that invited skiers to share in the development. For $1,000 a person received stock and lift privileges; for $5,000 in stock, the lease on a one-third-acre lot and two season lift passes.

"John was an Irish salesman, forceful and full of talk. His field was finance, and he was very enterprising. I knew that, compared to Squaw Valley, Alpine Meadows terrain was not as dramatic. There are no big peaks. You can't see the resort from the ground until you get to the actual base area. We knew that, because of the surrounding U.S. Forest land, there would never be homesites built to overlook the slopes. But what the area does have are great views and extremely appealing slopes for all levels of skiers. That's why I insisted we build our first lift all the way to the top. It was conceived as a family resort to be built by skiers for skiers."

Klaussen began his plans as a road was being built the three miles from Highway 89 to the base area. From the crest he designed a long run for novices on a trail wide and devoid of sharp corners that never dropped more than twelve percent. "The runs were fairly obvious. You had open bowls above and a meadow below. It was just a matter of connecting them. Monty Atwater and I would mark the trees to be cut. He'd go down one side of a slope and I'd be on the other. Instead of elaborate plans, topo maps and office studies, we just did it ourselves. We were both skiers and we knew what would make a good trail. We wanted good exposure so we designed a lot of the slopes from the northeast."

Klaussen took snow measurements and determined the height and placement of the lift towers for the Summit chair. He also chose the site for the lodge. "Monty thought the lodge should be built farther up the mountain, just under the breakover near Gunner's Knob. I wanted it much farther back, across the creek. We compromised and put it where it is now. In retrospect my idea would have been better as the resort grew up. But it was probably the best location at the time to start up the area."

It was during this time that Reily left the Carnation Company and promoted his dream full-time. He built a large redwood home just below the base area parking lots, and from there continued to take people into the area by snowcat in hopes of selling stock.

Bernie Pomagowski, manufacturer of Poma lifts, came to see Reily to view the new ski area. "Reily wanted to impress this guy, but it was really storming. John wasn't a person to take no for an answer. He packed him into the snowcat and off they went. The weather turns into a blizzard, and they're supposed to be back. Just before dark, as I'm going to look for them, here come two guys walking out of the snowstorm." Blinded by the storm, Reily had missed the bridge and dropped into a creek bed. Stuck, they had stumbled through heavy weather for two miles until finding a way out.

"John was a visionary.
He had an unshakable sense
about skiing.
He believed in John Muir,
about finding good things
in the mountains.
He probably could have
financed the smaller resort
he first had in mind.
In the end he lost control of
Alpine Meadows,
but never of his dreams.
He was always moving on to
some grander project.
His dream of a wonderful
family resort at
Alpine Meadows remains alive.
It's is a great place that has
brought a lot of pleasure
to many people."

"It really shows Reily's persistence. He wanted to get this person alone to sell him on the place, but Mr. Pomagowski was seventy-five years old. It really wasn't a smart thing to do. John, however, was on a mission." But despite his energy, Reily's efforts fell short. By 1960 he was still undercapitalized.

"The California Department of Corporations had set an amount of $750,000 to be raised before they'd release the fund. John had raised only half a million dollars in two years. He just couldn't sell it. That's when the Bear Creek Association got the idea of making up the difference and taking control."

Started by a trio of Alpine Meadows directors, Lawrence Metcalf, Byron Nishkian and William Evers, the Bear Creek Association was a mountain country club formed from the ranks of San Francisco socialites to help guarantee attendance on the Alpine Meadows slopes. Originally, the group planned to build its own rope tow along with other amenities such as tennis courts, an artificial lake and horse stables. With membership already reaching into the hundreds they purchased the rest of the stock.

"They got the right to a leased lot and ski privileges. They also got control." The Bear Creek Association ousted Reily as the corporation's president and replaced him with Byron Nishkian. "Reily knew what was going to happen. He'd had two years to raise the money and hadn't been able to do it. To his credit, he decided it was better to lose control than not do the ski resort at all. He still had a major portion of stock and his land. Still, his dream was shattered. It had slipped away."

Courtesy of Alpine Meadows

Peter Klaussen and John Reily in 1961.

With Nishkian's appointment as president, Klaussen's days as Alpine Meadows' general manager were numbered. He was asked to step down from the board of directors and demoted to mountain manager. Still, in just six months in 1961, Klaussen had created a ski resort from scratch: he built a Riblet double chair from the 6,920-foot base to Alpine's 8,450-foot summit; installed two Poma lifts to serve beginner slopes; cleared a 500-car parking lot; and began work on the day lodge.

"We would have completed the lodge before opening if Nishkian hadn't stepped in. It was budgeted at $110,000, but Nishkian tried cutting costs, and he redesigned the building. The concept of the building was changed from an A-frame with catchments for melt off to a barn. We lost the original architect, and the builder insisted on time and materials instead of a consolidated bid. The end result was that it was not completed until after the new year, at a final cost of $150,000."

Alpine Meadows opened December 28, 1961. The resort earned praise for its terrain. Famed skier Luggi Foeger, formerly of Badger Pass, was hired to run the ski school. The Lake Tahoe Ski Club made its headquarters there, adding community support. Klaussen directed avalanche safety and on-hill operations, including plowing of the road and parking lots. Yet in March 1962, before the completion of Alpine's first season, he was forced out.

"I thought I was supposed to run the ski area, but they obviously didn't see it that way. Luggi, who was only the ski school director, was allowed to make most of the decisions. My ideas were bypassed. I had been Reily's man, and that kind of summed it up."

Klaussen would continue in the ski industry as a consultant. In the mid-60s he made feasibility reports and developed plans for the creation of Northstar-at-Tahoe. He completed avalanche studies for Disney Corporation's proposed Independence Lake resort and helped plan the new Snowmass resort near Aspen, Colorado, as well as the Resort At Squaw Creek in Squaw Valley. During the 70s, he was assistant director of the Desert Research Institute in Nevada. With his wife Joan, he raised four children, two of whom raced at the national level, and found time to win ten National Masters ski racing championships.

Carson White, public relations director at Alpine Meadows, skiing down one of the runs designed by Peter Klaussen.

C H R I S

K U R A I S A

—

H E A V E N L Y

V A L L E Y

1 9 1 1 – 1 9 9 6

"My father brought our family
up to the lake
for a summer of camping.
I loved to fish.
I hiked every peak.
I absolutely fell in love
with the place.
I made up my mind
that I was going to live
at Lake Tahoe.
That was my dream."

hris Kuraisa first discovered Lake Tahoe when he was eleven, but it wasn't until 1953 at the age of forty-two that he fulfilled his dream. By that time, he'd already fit in several successful careers in the San Francisco Bay Area.

Lying about his age, he joined the National Guard at age fifteen and within a decade rose through the ranks to captain. A correspondence course got him a job at Standard Oil, and from 1937 to 1945 the Yugoslavian-born Kuraisa worked for its Richmond refinery as a master mechanic and engineer. He also simultaneously owned furniture-hauling, surplus supply and gas station businesses.

Highly motivated, he had an infectious energy that carried into sports. The six-foot-two, 200-pound athlete played semipro baseball on a hometown Oakland team. In his mid-twenties he took a liking to ice skating, began taking lessons and qualified to judge ice skating events. He also discovered skiing.

"I first tried skiing in 1938 at Silver Springs. I immediately became hooked. The following year I skied at Sugar Bowl as often as possible." Though successful and happily situated in Oakland, the mountains still beckoned. When the opportunity to buy a sporting goods store on the southeast corner of Lake Tahoe arose in 1953, Kuraisa sold his trucking business and moved to the mountains. "My wife, Dottie, had a lot of apprehension. We were doing pretty well. But before I married her, back when we were teenagers, I made her promise one day we'd move to Tahoe."

He sunk a major portion of his life savings into the business. Except for several casinos, few attractions drew tourists to the south shore of Lake Tahoe in the winter. Businesses operated during the summer, and the merchants saved enough to buy groceries during the lean winter months. To increase income, Kuraisa kept his store open any hour of the day or night if customers came calling. He also knew a bargain when it was presented. After chancing upon a close-out sale at a Bay Area skating rink, he purchased six hundred pairs of ice skates for $25 and started his own rink at Lake Tahoe. Not long after, local resident Bill Sutherland, a United Airlines pilot, offered Kuraisa the chance to buy a small ski area.

"Sutherland offered to sell me his two-rope tow area called the Bijou Ski Run for $1,950 and the property for another $3,750. I felt the ski area would complement the sport shop. Besides I loved to ski. A lot of people thought I was crazy. Skiing wasn't that big. When I told my wife what I'd done, she started crying. She said, 'You've spent all the eating money!'"

Adding to the pressure, there wasn't a flake on the ground into February. Yet Kuraisa was not discouraged. He told his wife not to worry, that it was going to snow. He was right. It snowed two feet the next day. The following Washington's Birthday weekend proved remarkably successful.

"It was really exciting. Dottie and some of her friends sold drinks and sandwiches. We pulled in $500 in three days and over $5,000 profit for the season. That was selling lift tickets for only a dollar!"

68

© Carolyn Caddes

"If you're honest, if you treat people right, you'll make friends and be successful.
I'd like to be remembered as a person who never cheated anybody out of a nickel."

However, he quickly learned that running a ski area left little time for skiing. He operated and maintained the rope tows, sold tickets and oversaw the day-to-day operations of his sporting goods store. Dottie helped out by operating a small restaurant at the ski area. "It was pretty hectic at times, but I love a challenge. I finally fitted the rope tows with electric motors, and we kept making money and new friends into the second year."

During the summer of 1954, Kuraisa climbed the surrounding peaks that overlooked his small ski area. He visualized a much bigger plan, one that could develop winter tourism for the area on a grander scale. "To me the geographical location was perfect. The views were captivating. From the air, the upper basin reminded me of a huge donut."

He concluded that the community could support year-round recreation. His dream reached fruition when he met and shared his ideas with prominent South Shore businessmen George Canon, Philip "Curly" Musso and Rudy Gersick. Kuraisa had already sketched a master plan for a ski area that stretched to the top of Monument Peak and he obtained a U. S. Forest Service use permit. He also purchased close to 200 acres from John Keller for a base area. From there he would build a 1,600-foot vertical lift up to the 8,100-foot elevation saddle that faced Lake Tahoe.

His business partners thought he was corny for naming it "Heavenly Valley." Kuraisa insisted that the name would draw attention to the upper basin of the mountain where long boulevards of intermediate terrain overlooked majestic views of Lake Tahoe. "Originally, my long-range plan called for incorporating the Nevada side of the mountain with a gondola from the town of Genoa to the top of Monument Peak and another tramway from where it is now. I had a lot of ideas, but I knew the key to our success would be having a lift going to the top, winter or summer, for sightseeing and sports activity."

Armed with plan and permit, a financial partnership was formed among the four men with Kuraisa as majority owner. They hired Lutz Aynedter, a ski instructor from nearby Edelweiss ski area, to help map out slope design under the resort's first chair. When Aynedter looked down the steep fall line, he told Kuraisa that it was like looking down the barrel of a gun. Said Kuraisa, "You've just named the run!"

The owners contracted with Heron Lift Engineering to build Chair One, the "Gunbarrel Chair." Kuraisa and his workers erected twenty-six towers for the chairlift in eight days and poured the supporting concrete for the counterweight in less than a month. With two chainsaws, Kuraisa and his friend Shelton Varney cut trees and cleared the Gunbarrel slope and sold the timber to a logging company for $18,000.

Heavenly Valley opened December 15, 1955 with two feet of snow on the ground. The community was out in force, along with media and a throng of skiers. However, Kuraisa wasn't there. Two days before, his eleven-year-old son, Eddie, was killed by a passing car while riding his bicycle. "I talked to George Canon. I told him to open it up, and that once things settled down, I'd be back."

Struggling through the tragedy, Kuraisa overcame his grief and returned to guide Heavenly Valley to a successful reality. In the following years, he gradually added more lifts to the upper regions of the mountain that straddled the border of California and Nevada. Summers became as successful as winters. Tourists rode the lift to the upper terminal for the panoramic views of Lake Tahoe, and many stayed at the top for a steak dinner at the Pioneer Hut. "We sold peanuts to tourists to feed the chipmunks. It was so successful that it paid the costs for summer operation alone."

The opening of the Lake Tahoe Airport brought commercial flights to South Shore and tourism swelled. Traditionally conservative bankers began to look at Heavenly, not as a fringe activity, but as a sound business venture. "We never put another nickel of our own money into the resort again. We were making money hand over fist. The place went crazy. We could get a loan for the next lift with a simple phone call."

Success did not make Kuraisa overlook his local community. He set up school programs and, working with school administrators, gave free ski passes to families that could not afford them so that "every kid could ski in that valley whether he could afford it or not."

When Kuraisa hired Stein Eriksen to help promote Heavenly Valley, the resort gained increasing national prominence. Eriksen sponsored international ski races, special events and even beauty pageants such as the "Miss Snow Fun" contest. He entertained patrons with his acrobatics, doing daily flips on his skis off "Stein's Rock," and promoted weekly "Stein Slalom" races.

Courtesy of Carson White

Stein Ericksen

Although Eriksen moved on after two years at Heavenly Valley, Kuraisa's drive and imagination continued to make its mark. In 1962 he placed the resort securely in the top tier of international ski resorts by initiating the construction of the largest aerial tramway in North America. "From the beginning I wanted a tramway at Heavenly. We were selling a lot of tickets to sightseers. To accommodate all the business, it was time to build something really special."

Heron Lift Engineering, which had constructed North America's first aerial tramway at Berthoud Pass, Colorado, was given the contract to build the twin 25-passenger cabins. To finance the project, Kuraisa joined forces with two new partners, Bob Wood and Dave Gay. "I basically negotiated a lease agreement where I would set up everything, and they would pay for it and own it. They got all the foot traffic and the resort got to use it for free."

By 1964 the hours it took to run the resort became too much for Kuraisa. "I had worked hard, and I was getting burned out. The exciting part had been putting it together, taking a raw mountain from nothing and watching it grow. I'd promised my wife we'd travel and do other things. It had come time to get out." He sold his 40 percent share of Heavenly Valley to the company attorney, Hugh Killebrew, and his limited partners.

Retirement didn't slow Kuraisa down. He continued to ski up to 100 days a year and became a certified instructor. At age 58, he took up tennis, passed his instructor's certificate and worked at Vic Braden tennis camps. By the late 1970s, he was a line judge for top professional matches.

He continued to keep his hand in the ski business, consulting for ski resorts such as Sugar Bowl and Mount Rose. "I had it all lined up to buy Slide Mountain, Sky Tavern, Mount Rose and Ski Incline. I had the opportunity to tie them together. I also had the permits to build a gondola from Highway 395 in Carson City to the base of Slide. It really would have been unique. However, it didn't happen. My agreement with Heavenly prevented me from opening a ski area within fifty miles of Lake Tahoe."

Kuraisa continued to stay active in a variety of hobbies and business ventures until his unexpected death in November 1996.

Within ten years after taking over the tiny Bijou Ski Run, Kuraisa had created one of North America's premier resorts. Heavenly Valley's popularity helped to make the Tahoe Basin a year-round vacation Mecca.

Courtesy of Carson White

George Canon, Philip "Curly" Musso, and Rudy Gersick join Chris Kuraisa (right) at the top of Gunbarrel Chair.

*"I always saw the sport
through my children's and
now through the eyes of
my grandchildren.
Skiing is a great family sport,
clean-aired and healthy,
something to do
with the children."*

Most Kirkwood skiers would not recognize Bud Klein, the modest, self-effacing founder of the ski area. Despite his prominence as head of a multimillion-dollar empire with major interests in banking, steel, recreation and agriculture, the Stanford-educated, Stockton-based Klein keeps a low profile. Dealing with his business interests prevents him from becoming a fixture on Kirkwood trails; however he is, in a way, always present. Kirkwood is not so much the culmination of his dream as the completion of a family odyssey.

"All four of my children skied. They got me into the sport." Lean and athletic, Klein, who played volleyball for the United States at the 1956 Pan American Games, looks like he could keep up with his grandchildren.

His gentle demeanor and laid-back drawl belies a steely resolve. Though he didn't know much about the ski industry at first, he did know what he liked and disliked. Traveling from Stockton with his family to Tahoe's larger and more acclaimed resorts, Klein, an avid skier, became increasingly lukewarm towards his skiing experience.

"Sometimes trails were confusing and packed full of crowds. It was tough keeping an eye on my children, especially at the bottom of the mountain. It was a zoo-like atmosphere on the weekends. I kept thinking how nice it would be to have an area that kids and parents could ski together without so much worry or hassle."

In 1965 Klein first visited the Kirkwood valley while accompanying his friend Bruce Orvis, a fourth generation San Joaquin Valley rancher, on an inspection of his cattle grazing in the meadow beneath Thimble Peak. "I thought it was the most beautiful spot on earth. It was inspiring. I fell in love with the place." He studied the alpine meadow surrounded on three sides by spectacular slopes creating a natural amphitheater. The valley floor rested at 7,800 feet elevation. Thimble Peak's crest dominated the landscape at 9,850 feet ensuring both quantity and quality of snow. However, he wasn't the first to eye Kirkwood as a ski area.

Tahoe National Forest winter recreation specialist Monty Atwater had conducted a helicopter and ground study in 1963 of possible ski resort sites in the El Dorado National Forest. Thimble Peak was the survey team's first choice among the areas investigated. They liked the ridge's north-facing aspect, slope protection and minimal tree clearing requirements.

Isolation, however, was a major stumbling block. While Kirkwood was near Lake Tahoe, and easily accessed by Highway 88, the route was closed in winter. Klein remembers riding a snowcat into the area during the winter of 1968 for a snow survey. "We stayed at the Kirkwood Inn, but first we had to find the place. There was so much snow we had to probe down to the top of the inn. We dug in finally and lived in the building that was like an igloo for eight days."

© Carolyn Caddes

"I still see skiing through the eyes of kids. Kirkwood is truly a family mountain resort.

When you arrive at Kirkwood, you've arrived at a special place.

Kirkwood has a great future. It's a painting I want to finish."

The Kirkwood Inn, once a way station for travelers in the 1860s, and later a haven for hunters and fishermen, was one of the few buildings in the valley. There were no power, water or sewer lines. Before Klein could think of operating lifts, the ski resort would have to become a self-contained community with diesel-generated power, complete with a water and sewage system.

"Everybody thought I was crazy, including my family. It was quite an undertaking. I knew I was sticking my neck out, but I really wanted to make it work. I found Stockton businessmen who were also intrigued by Kirkwood's potential." They formed the Kirkwood Meadows Corporation and embarked on the development process; obtaining an option on the Kirkwood land, conducting studies, and negotiating a trade for the surrounding Forest Service land. It took five years.

"At first, I thought I would just be a financier and Kirkwood sort of a hobby," Klein, who was the project's largest investor, says. "It became a very consuming business venture that took a lot of thought and a lot of money."

To make Highway 88 an all-weather road, Klein and his associates posted a $700,000 cash bond and signed a cooperative agreement with the California Highway Department to build two maintenance stations between Carson Pass and Peddler Hill. Early plans called for a $42 million ski facility which escalated to over $55 million. When permits to build a ski resort on public land were granted by the U.S. Forest Service in August 1971, the Kirkwood partners found themselves battling a lawsuit by the Sierra Club which opposed the incorporation of Thimble Peak into the development.

"Our original goal that remains unchanged is a desire to commit as little offense to nature as possible while developing a sense of being in a special place. We wanted slow growth with a quality ski area." After nearly a year, the court ruled in favor of Kirkwood. But that was just the beginning. To carve a first-rate resort out of such primitive wilderness was going to be an arduous task.

Through the efforts of Janek Kunczynski, one of Kirkwood's original directors and the owner of Lift Engineering, Dick Reuter was lured from Squaw Valley to become the infant resort's mountain manager. "We hired Dick Reuter because of his reputation for making a mountain work. Thank goodness he came and stayed. He gave us a lot of knowledge and he gave us 110 percent every day. He argued where to place the chairs. I know that without Dick, Kirkwood would have never been as successful."

Boasting the highest base elevation in Northern California, Kirkwood opened in December 1972 with four chairlifts, a 15,000-square-foot lodge, employee housing, a sewage system and a power-generating facility.

"What I had in mind was a family ski area that would be pristine and never become a massive thing. It was a family deal. I knew because of where it was situated it would never be that profitable but always successful. The main goal was to build something special."

"We had a lot of problems, but a lot of success the first year. Parking was limited, but the mountain could easily handle over 2,000 skiers. People really enjoyed the friendly atmosphere, but the lack of water has always hurt us. We could never make snow and the drought years killed us."

Changes came gradually to Kirkwood. It survived the drought years of the mid-70s, and Klein's acumen as secretary-treasurer kept it growing. By its tenth anniversary the ski resort offered 2,000 acres, nine lifts and abundant runs. However, in 1994 it was necessary for the partners to file for consensual Chapter 11 bankruptcy reorganization. "We got into financial trouble. Some of the original shareholders didn't want to meet increasing monetary requirements. We needed new financing."

A year later both the Telluride Ski and Golf Company and Charles Cobb, former CEO of Arvida/Disney Corporation, purchased significant interests in Kirkwood. The change of ownership launched the ski area into a new phase of development. Klein, who remains a major investor of Kirkwood, acknowledges the hardscrabble years, the hard work, and the heartache of seeing a dream unfold. "We had several options. I know we went with the right group. Kirkwood will maintain the character of the valley and its natural setting."

Courtesy of Kirkwood Ski Resort

Kids enjoying the slopes at Kirkwood.

*"When I was twelve years old
growing up in Nebraska,
my Dad lost his crops.
We drove out West in 1936,
came over Donner Summit
in his 1928 Essex headed for
farmland around Chico.
We'd have to stop to pour
water in the radiator.
It gave me time to look around.
I liked those mountains."*

Dick Reuter dreamed about mountains as a boy growing up on the plains of Nebraska but he never thought he would see them, except in books. When the family drove west in 1936, the family's fortune consisted of $40 in his father's pocket. Those were hard times, but it didn't stop the young plainsman from his dream of living in the high country.

He got his chance after seeing action in France during World War II and heading straight toward those mountains he'd first seen as a kid. "I'd made up my mind during the war. I was logging for an outfit below Lassen Park and running trap lines. This Indian friend gave me a pair of 11-foot skis made out of red fir. They were real wide and big sticks, but I loved them."

He finally got a winter job running a rope tow on the lower slopes of Mount Lassen. Shortly after, in 1955, he drifted into the Tahoe Basin and began working at Squaw Valley as a ski patrolman. He lived his first year in the first aid room, complete with leaky roof, but he'd found a home, one that lasted seventeen years.

"Before Monty Atwater came to Squaw Valley in 1957 with modernized snow safety techniques, we used to ski avalanches off. We'd work in pairs, roped together. One fellow would belay the other onto a slope to see what would happen. We used to ride Chair One with the Headwall above looking you right in the eye. We started up the jigback tram in first gear. At that speed it would take an hour to get to the top."

All alone, without radios, avalanche-locating beacons or snowcats, Reuter admits that he was living dangerously. A true storyteller, he tells of his experiences that reveal a gentle but determined personality for whom obstacles could be overcome with just common sense and hard work. He has needed those strengths because Mother Nature has not always been kind.

"Once I was ski-checking Headwall and it climaxed, sounded like a box of powder going off. A Class Five slide unloaded down the face of Headwall and rumbled for over a mile past mid-mountain destroying the bottom terminal of Cornice Two lift and the top lift shack of Cornice One. I was caught up in it and thought to myself, I wasn't going to come out of it this time, when the damn thing popped me out like a pumpkin seed. I think I limped away from that one. It taught me a lot of respect for avalanches."

It wasn't necessarily less dangerous for Reuter as mountain manager of Squaw Valley. In 1970 he came close to death after falling from a lift tower while repairing a cable during a storm. Dropping sixty feet, he landed on a snowcat. The fall crushed his chest and pushed his ribs into his lungs.

"They told me I was not going to live one more day if they didn't try this never-before-performed operation. This fellow went in there and cut out part of my lung, then wired all my ribs and zipped me up. I still got the metal inside." He spent twenty-eight days in a Reno hospital but within the year he was back climbing lift towers.

© Carolyn Caddes

"I've always kept in mind that nature and the great outdoors don't play any favorites. Mother Nature always has the last say.
We've had a perfect snow safety record at Kirkwood since day one, but it could end tomorrow.
I tell the boys never to get cocky, never take anything for granted."

After seventeen years at Squaw Valley, Reuter accepted an offer of a job at Kirkwood ski area. "It was quite a gamble to take over as mountain manager here at Kirkwood in 1972. I could see they had more than a share of problems. It would be a challenge. It was also going to be hard on my family. I had four kids and a wife, but there were too many people at Squaw Valley."

That summer Reuter began trail clearing. The resort opened to a record cold winter. He discovered frequent winds of over 100 miles an hour that swept the upper ridges bare. The lodge and support buildings were not finished, so he set up his mechanics shop in an abandoned barn.

On the mountain he sometimes used over 200 charges to control avalanches and protect the power house and lifts. Reuter's nearly two decades of experience with avalanches were invaluable for keeping nature's threats at bay. "I'd say I've been lucky through the years. I've played some hunches correctly which have saved me."

The next year Reuter convinced the resort owners to install two more chairs to access the top of the mountain. He built a garage for vehicles and set up a military cannon to support his avalanche control program.

"The new chairs got us going. People started coming. Things got sorted out. I was lucky. Some real tough guys came to work for me. Now I look up and see all those trails and people having fun, and I'm kinda proud of it all. The lifts have improved so, and the grooming is really amazing. The progress isn't through yet."

In 1990, at age sixty-eight, Dick Reuter retired and went back to logging. "I always did prefer the woods. Less people you know, but I had a wife, so I needed a year-round job. I have to admit I miss the ski operations though, but I also know I got out at the right time. In today's ski resort a mountain manager has to spend more time in an office. I was always outside seeing that the work was being done. You see, I told my kids, 'Do what you want to do in life. Don't get a job. Do the kind of job you like.' Unfortunately my kids took me at my word. I got three of them working in the ski industry. They love the mountains more than me."

" I could see that I'd gotten myself into an interesting situation, but I'm bullheaded. I stuck with her. The skiing was good. It's really a smaller version of Squaw Valley with great snow conditions."

Setting the first lift towers at Kirkwood in 1972.

Above Donner Ski Ranch.

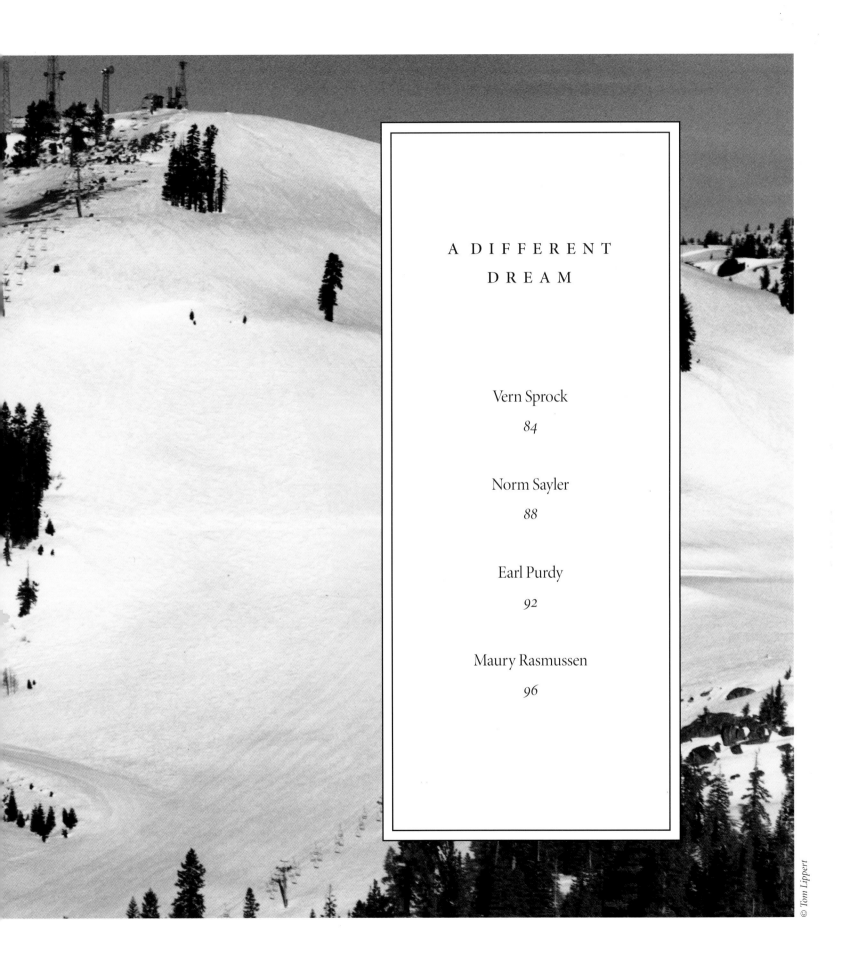

A DIFFERENT DREAM

© Tom Lippert

*"The location of (the original)
Sierra Ski Ranch was actually a
poor place to build a ski resort.
There was no flat area at the
bottom, and it received minimal
snowfall compared to other
spots, but it was popular.
The parking lot was always full,
people enjoyed themselves, and
the idea was to make a living so
we could stay in the mountains
and still eat."*

For forty years, Vern Sprock made it a point to accompany his Sierra Ski Ranch ski patrol on sweep for the last run of the day. "It was always to get the cobwebs out. Business had to wait until after five o'clock. Some people growled because I was never in the office during the day, but that's not what running a ski resort is about."

A lot of snow has fallen over Echo Summit since the late 1940s when Sprock first began building one of Tahoe's ski area gems. "Sierra Ski Ranch was actually started by two brothers, Ray and Floyd Barrett, in 1946. I first worked for them in the late forties, then took over the operation in 1953."

Raised in the Sacramento Valley, Sprock received his first taste of mountain life in 1938. At eighteen he got a job running trap lines and working at Saddlebag Lake Resort near Yosemite's Tioga Pass. His first skis were seven feet long with toe straps for bindings. "My father was a farmer and he thought I was crazy going to the mountains. To me, the high country was big and wild. It was an interesting lifestyle. I returned to the Sierra Nevada after World War II. My brother-in-law owned a small store and restaurant on a piece of property along Highway 50 at Echo Summit. There wasn't much going on, just a lot of beautiful country with a series of post offices in between. If you needed a doctor, you drove thirty miles to Placerville. But I met my wife, Bobbie, on Echo Summit, and I fell in love with the area, too."

After the two were married they decided to join her brother at Echo Summit. "There wasn't much of a population on the summit, but there was plenty of snowfall. A small group of owner-operated ski resorts such as Edelweiss, Needlehorn and Strawberry sprang up along Highway 50 leading into the Tahoe Basin." Vern and Bobbie decided to buy into a little ski area.

In 1955 Sprock replaced one of his area's two rope tows with a Poma lift, which increased the resort's vertical drop to 350 feet and expanded his base operation, but he was looking for something bigger than the 80 acres of terrain he managed. Skiing the ridges above his ski area he found a mantled geography dominated by thick forests of ponderosa pine and fir that shielded fresh snow from harsh winter winds. Most of the terrain contained modest, long pitches. From the top of its 8,852-foot summit, he discovered spectacular views of emerald-hued Lake Tahoe.

"I explored the area with the Forest Service. CalTrans wanted to buy the land where the original Sierra Ski Ranch was situated to widen Highway 50. The Forest Service agreed we could move up there to continue the business."

Armed with a master plan and $600,000 in financing from a bank loan and the CalTrans buyout, Sprock opened the new Sierra Ski Ranch on Christmas Day 1968. The ski area offered one Poma, a rope tow, one chairlift and a 10,000-square-foot day lodge. The opening also coincided with a winter of record snowfall. When the three miles of unpaved road into the resort became too muddy, Sprock towed cars in and out. Winter storms knocked trees across his chairlift

© Carolyn Caddes

"Growing up as a kid I never thought about living in the mountains.
It wasn't until I got here that I didn't want to leave.
Skiing gave me a place to live."

and rope tow, and the road over Echo Summit leading to Lake Tahoe's South Shore was closed frequently with heavy snows.

"We had plenty of problems, but nothing we couldn't fix with some hard work. There was no stopping. I'd found a spot in the mountains where I wanted to live and I was determined to get it going. It had great ski terrain and we were doing something that gave people a lot of enjoyment."

By the mid-70s Sierra Ski Ranch was succeeding beyond his expectations. The resort made money every year, enough that Sprock never again went to a bank to finance new projects, relying instead on resort profits and his own money from a summer construction business to install new chairlifts.

"We put in probably the first chairlift just for beginners. Eventually, we replaced it with a detachable quad complete with tower and terminal adjustments so entry-level skiers, who sometimes have a phobia about heights, could be closer to the snow. We invested a lot of effort with grooming and were innovative with our children's ski school. We always looked for new things, something state of the art, so people knew we were always moving forward."

In 1977, when the Forest Service permitted an increase in skier capacity from 2,500 to 7,000, Sierra Ski Ranch began hosting more than 300,000 skiers a season. To keep up with demand, Sprock, under a Forest Service agreement, designed more runs.

"I was scouting out new trails with a Forest Service ranger. We skied down a narrow, steep-sided gully that gave way to a great slope through trees. The ranger commented that this slope had always been a favorite spot of a minister from Placerville who frequented the resort. We named the slope 'Preacher's Passion' in his honor."

With wife Bobbie running the front office and children Peter and Kathy as department heads, Sierra Ski Ranch became a family-run venture. Orienting their resort towards the skiing family, Sprock made tough operational decisions, even refusing to sell alcohol or encourage its consumption on resort property. "We never had problems on the slopes as a result from drinking. It was the same with snowboarders. Only after studying the product did I eventually allow them on the mountain."

Sprock's hands-on approach didn't come without a price. In January 1975 while fixing a drive terminal on one of his lifts, Sprock slipped and caught his leg in the universal joint of the drive line between the motor and gear case.

"The leg was nearly torn off, only a little bit of tissue held it on. It took awhile to get me out of it. I was able to disassemble part of the machinery, then I wilted."

After five operations and six weeks in a hospital bed, Sprock began his recuperation. "There was never any thought of getting out of the business. I had to get back on the hill. That's all there was to it." Two years later Sprock donned a pair of skis and went skiing.

"You have to do what you feel is correct. We proved the resort could be popular without an après-ski mentality. We never wanted to deny recreation to anyone, but we looked to what skiing was all about."

"Randy Watson was my doctor. He saved my life and stayed close to me during my struggle. The first time I went skiing again he came out with me. A week later he came back to see how I was doing. I learned a lot about life from him. He wanted to see me, not talk on the phone. I realized that you can listen all you want, trust whomever, but you still have to see things for yourself."

Although the ankle and leg remain stiff, Sprock still skis as often as possible. "As long as there is a mountain to ski to get the cobwebs out, you'll find me out on the hill."

Sprock dreamed for more Sierra Ski Ranch expansion. In 1988, lacking slopeside lodging, Sprock proposed a $100 million project that called for ten more lifts, fifteen miles of new ski runs and hotel accommodations on 1,570 acres of national forest property.

"It was a good proposal and one that would have placed Sierra Ski Ranch in the upper echelon of North American ski resorts. We addressed all the questions raised, but in the general environmental climate, it could not be resolved."

After several years of surveys and impact studies, the Forest Service denied Sprock the necessary permits. He sold Sierra Ski Ranch to Trimont Corporation in 1993, which renamed the area Sierra-at-Tahoe.

"The challenge wasn't there anymore. I had done just about everything I could, and looking back, there isn't much I would have changed. It's a top notch ski area." Sprock was awarded the Charley Proctor Award by the North American Ski Journalists Association in 1990 for his contribution to skiing.

Courtesy of Vern and Bobbie Sprock

Vern and Bobbie Sprock with their children, Kathy and Peter, who worked at Sierra Ski Ranch from the time they were old enough to clean the toilets at the end of the day. Bobbie commented that she wished all her employees were as conscientious as her kids.

NORM SAYLER
—
DONNER SKI RANCH

"Sure, it takes perseverance. Even today, after forty years, it is still a day-to-day struggle. But skiing is a great life. If you're able to choose your lifestyle, why not make it enjoyable. I never thought that much about money. I never expected to make any, but what a choice to live this sort of life."

orm Sayler bristles at the thought of changing anything about Donner Ski Ranch. "I'm like the guy who continues to drive his old car forever. I don't need a new car. I like mine just the way it is."

Donner Ski Ranch is no architectural marvel. There is nothing fancy about the modest, slopeside lodge with a semi-claustrophobic cafeteria area where guests are encouraged to meet each other. There's a cozy upstairs bar where Sayler claims the corner table as his office. He likes to check out the action on the main slope served by his latest pride: a fixed-grip triple chair.

"I'm called a dinosaur of the industry because I've failed to keep up with changes attracting skiers to resorts elsewhere. However, I can't think of being anywhere else."

Sayler's ski area is undoubtedly the last of its kind. Donner Ski Ranch's simplicity and affordable costs continue to make it a little gem of Tahoe ski resorts with terrain that features a balanced variety of steeps to rolling shoulders. Despite the high technology that has transformed skiing into one simply of bottom-line profits, Sayler and his staff offer a kind of product that harkens back to a former era birthed by exuberant outdoorsmen.

"The marketing people have decided that today's industry, all the high-speed stuff and other toys, are what people want. They think they can show you what's fun. Well, guess what? There are some skiers who don't want it, who don't care about that stuff."

Skiing and fun have been synonymous with Sayler since he first began taking day trips with his church group to the Sierra Nevada in the 1940s. "It was at Cisco Grove. I went right up the rope tow and came right down. From then on, I was a skier."

He moved permanently to Donner Summit in 1954. By then, rated a Class A ski racer, Sayler trained with Olympian Dick Buek. Dick's father Carl allowed Sayler to live in his family's garage in exchange for cleaning the day lodge the Bueks operated at Soda Springs. To supplement a very meager income, Sayler remembers digging through the old couches of the Soda Springs Hotel every Sunday after the weekend ski crowds departed. "It's surprising how many coins you could find. Back then I did whatever it took. I'd shovel snow, bootpack slopes, wash dishes, anything to earn a lift ticket. I was hooked on skiing. It was my way of life."

Sayler's first real job was as a laborer, digging tower holes for the first chairlift at Donner Ski Ranch in the summer of 1955. The following year he began a two-year stint in the Army, assigned to the mountain troops in Colorado. "It was grand. All my race buddies were in the same outfit: Chuck Lewis who started Copper Mountain, Tom Dempsey who helped build Mammoth and Buddy Werner. I got to meet a lot of the upstarts of the ski industry."

He got married and returned to Donner Summit to accept the position of general manager at Donner Ski Ranch. He's never looked back. "I wanted to raise a family. They offered me $300 a month plus a place to stay. I thought it was a pretty good deal."

© Carolyn Caddes

"My philosophy is simple. I don't show people how to have fun.
I let people have fun. That's what skiing is about."

By 1961 Sayler began purchasing stock in the ski resort. "I didn't have much money. Some of the stockholders really wanted out. I was able to buy my first 500 shares for twenty-five cents a share!" Stockholders Byron Nishkian and Larry Metcalf sold their interest in Donner Ski Ranch to invest in the Bear Creek Association in Alpine Meadows. Within a few years, Sayler became the majority stockholder.

When Interstate 80 was completed in 1965, the old Donner Summit highway (U.S. 40) and Donner Ski Ranch were bypassed as travelers chose the fastest route to Squaw Valley and Lake Tahoe. The lively business district between Soda Springs and Donner Lake with several gasoline stations, hotels, restaurants and bars slowly faded away, leaving the area to 400 hardy year-round residents. Norm remembers one year when the lack of snow added to the summit area's economic plight. "After some early rains there wasn't a cloud in the sky until March. We took in $17,000 for the whole season." However, to Sayler, who considers his mountain his best friend, it's all part of the game.

He counts many firsts in skiing that derived from his pursuit of fun. "We were the first to offer night skiing. Back in 1958 I strung 100-watt lights on the rope tow. It might not have been too sophisticated, but people were out there having a ball." Sayler and Olympian Tom Corcoran set and competed in one of the first dual giant slaloms in the late 1950s. When telemarkers were not allowed at other ski resorts, they found a home at Donner Ski Ranch, and Sayler was the first to allow disabled skiers an opportunity to play on the ski slopes. He says he was the first to run programs for women and for youths, busing children from Sacramento to Donner Ski Ranch on the weekends. "It was so popular it got too big for us. I finally handed the program over to a bigger resort."

When snowboarding arrived, Sayler immediately embraced the discipline, accepting boarders without hesitation. "Some resorts didn't allow them. Others made these people get special licenses. They looked like they were enjoying the snow to me. They bought a ticket. Why not let them on the slopes?"

Sayler recounts the time Dick Barrymore contacted him. The legendary filmmaker was having trouble finding a location to film a dangerous stunt. No resort would give him permission on their mountain because of the liability.

"Frankie Bear was going to do some triple twisting inverted somersault. I told Dick, 'Let's do it!' A week later this comical guy shows up in a Lincoln wearing a bearskin coat. He and I built a jump. He pulls the stunt off on the first attempt, gets back in his Lincoln and leaves. Years later he called me and said, 'Norm, you were crazy to let me do that.' I didn't think I was crazy. I thought it was pretty neat."

Sayler remains enthusiastic about the sport that has been his lifeblood. To him, it was all luck at every turn. Most of his success came from being in the right place at the right time. That and a bit of hard work.

"I'm the first to arrive every morning. I plow the parking lot myself. I can watch the groomers and see that the job is being done. I know when the cook showed up because I plowed his parking spot. I can see the whole resort in front of me beginning to wake up. I guess you could say I really do run this place by the seat of my pants."

He acknowledges that his ski area can't compete with some of his neighbors who offer more amenities to a demanding public. Nonetheless, he sees a bright future for his resort. "I hope this place will be here 100 years from now. I let people accept who we are. Not everybody wants a four-lane highway. They like these little back roads. I say, 'Come and share a fun day.' Being in the mountains, on the hill, are we lucky, or what?"

Courtesy of William B. Berry

Norm Sayler preparing to carry the Olympic Torch to Squaw Valley in 1960, shares the moment with Bill Berry who is covering the event for the press.

" The most important skill my father had was people skills. He had a talent for choosing key people to run the different resort departments. He had genuine concern for people and instilled in his employees a sincerity for the customer, to make them feel welcome. The customer came first,"
says son, Ralph.

n 1947 Earl Purdy was drinking a cup of coffee in a grocery store in the town of Long Barn when neighbors casually mentioned that the U.S. Forest Service had begun soliciting bids for development of a ski area at nearby Dodge Ridge. On a whim, Purdy added his name to the prospectus.

"He put his name down along with a $100 fee and forgot about it," says son, George Purdy. "Three months later the Forest Service contacted my father to see if he was interested. They'd rejected the other bidders. They had studied his business history and chosen him. It was something of a shock."

A former teacher, truck driver, highway patrolman and professional violinist, with a degree in architecture, Earl Purdy was operating a profitable general store and gas station between the towns of Ripon and Manteca called Simm's Station. Now, by chance, he'd stumbled upon the final venture of his multifaceted life.

"He'd been looking for a new business, something in the mountains to be closer to his family. He no longer enjoyed the commute to his store. He didn't know a lot about the ski industry but, of course, at that time not too many people did," says George, who is an employee of Dodge Ridge. "He had a lot of energy and common sense, and he was going back to the mountains."

Purdy had only picked up the sport of skiing in his 40s when his children began to take lessons. The only ski areas he knew were the nearby, single-surface lift resorts of Cold Stream, Little Sweden and Cottage Springs that catered to enthusiasts from Modesto and Lodi. "He'd ski even though he didn't know how," says youngest son Ralph. "The only way he could stop was to fall."

Purdy, nevertheless, had a penchant for challenge and an eye on the future. Combined with his fondness for mountain life and sense of community, he became the driving force for an awakening sport that helped change Tuolumne County into one of California's popular recreational spots.

Born in 1907, Purdy was raised on the family ranch in the small town of Kaweah outside Sequoia National Park. Purdy's father, a forest ranger and surveyor, introduced his son Earl to the outdoors at an early age. "My grandfather was responsible for drawing the first topographical maps of the Mineral King and Kings Canyon areas," says Ralph, a professor at University of California, Irvine. "My father accompanied him along with pack animals on many of the surveys."

During the 1930s Purdy drove deep into the Sierra near Sonora Pass to fish the rivers. He hiked the Dodge Ridge area, then called Lava Ridge, a name it was given because of the andesite lava flows that formed the landscape. From its rocky heights the terrain gave way to thick forests of Bennett junipers, the largest and oldest known specimen of western juniper. On clear days, from the ridge's 8,200-foot summit, he could spot the high reaches of Mount Diablo.

Historical photo courtesy of Ralph Purdy

*"He loved the mountains and the ski business," says son, Ralph. "His reward was going to work.
He liked people. He was always looking out for the public and the betterment of the community.
It was the most enjoyable part of his life. He'd always ask, 'Are we having fun?'"*

When Purdy's wife Mary and son George both developed asthma and needed a change of climate, Purdy, who felt attached to the Sonora Pass area, moved his family to the town of Long Barn, 25 miles below Dodge Ridge next to Stanislaus National Forest. "High enough to get out of the foxtails, low enough to escape the severe winters," he once explained in an interview.

Before accepting the option for the use permit from the Forest Service, Purdy undertook a three-month tour of ski resorts to decide for certain if skiing was a viable economic product. He traveled to Sun Valley. He visited Mammoth and Squaw Valley, two resorts in the early stages of operation. The more he traveled, the more he saw the possibilities for Dodge Ridge. After driving more than 5,000 miles he became sure of two things: He would develop the ski area and it had to have a chairlift.

"After Dad got back, he went out to the ski area and studied the terrain," remembers Ralph. "He pulled out a matchbook and opened it. He then sketched out everything that was going to be the ski resort. All along, while driving from ski resort to ski resort, he had in his mind what Dodge Ridge was going to look like. And when the final project was completed, it looked exactly like the layout on the matchbook."

Financial backing came from family members and additional investors from the Stockton area who recognized the benefits of winter recreation atop Sonora Pass. Once Purdy arranged a lease with the government, he began construction. During the summer, 27 million board feet of timber was cut clearing runs and three double rope tows were placed on varying slopes. Bob Heron, who had installed the chairlift at Squaw Valley, was chosen to construct the Dodge Ridge chair for $95,000.

Courtesy of Dodge Ridge

Dodge Ridge, 1956.

In all, the initial investment came to $250,000. In addition to the chair and surface lifts, the facilities included a 700-car parking lot and two-story day lodge, complete with ski shop and dining room, but without an après-ski cocktail bar. "We're only interested in family trade and the outdoorsy crowd," explained Purdy to critics.

Three thousand skiers flocked to Dodge Ridge on its opening day in 1950. Tickets sold at three dollars for an all-day lift pass and one dollar for a rope tow pass. Within a two-month ski season, it attracted 19,000 skiers. The next year numbers increased to 25,000 and Dodge Ridge became consistently profitable. Until he sold the resort in 1977, Purdy reported only one bad year—1963—when snow didn't arrive until March.

Purdy stressed a cautious approach to capital improvements. He never built housing facilities, relying on accommodations in the immediate area to take care of demands. Over the succeeding years, the resort added lifts and expanded facilities only as its income warranted them. More than ten years passed after the opening date before he installed a second chairlift. In 1968 Dodge Ridge completed a $300,000 expansion which included two new double chairlifts and the first section of a new 16,000-square-foot lodge.

"My father believed in growing without getting into debt. Eventually the resort fell behind the faster-growing resorts in California, but it never had money problems like some of those places," says Ralph.

In addition to running Dodge Ridge, Purdy helped found a group called Sonora Pass Vacationland that publicized Tuolumne County throughout Northern California. He sat on the committee to build the Sonora Bypass, was on the Tuolumne Regional Water District Board of Directors, president of the National Forest Recreation Association and director of the California Chamber of Commerce.

"People wanted him to run for state senate, but he felt an obligation to his ski resort. He was always very public-minded, nevertheless," says George.

At age seventy Purdy finally decided to sell Dodge Ridge. "It wasn't easy for him to stop. He was the type to go out on the hill every day to stay in touch with everything," says Ralph. "But it was time. He'd promised my mother they'd travel, and the ski industry was changing." After consulting at Dodge Ridge for two years for new owner Frank Helm, Purdy remained active in the communities surrounding Tuolumne County until his death in 1991.

*"To my father, problems were
something not to fight
but to handle in stride.
He never swore.
He always seemed to find
a solution."*

aury Rasmussen was approached in 1958 by his friend Bruce Orvis, a fourth generation San Joaquin Valley rancher, and asked to take a raw, bare mountain in a virtually roadless section of the High Sierra near Ebbetts Pass and turn it into a major ski area. Within weeks, the ardent outdoorsman, at age forty-eight, sold his lumber mill and packed his family up to the mountains.

"My father had a reputation for getting things done. That's why they came to him to help build a ski area," says son, Dennis Rasmussen. "He liked a challenge and he loved the mountains. To him, it wasn't that tough a decision to become involved with the project." Orvis and his partners invited Rasmussen to become director of Alpine Snow Bowl, a new corporation created to develop the Bear Valley-Mount Reba area.

Rasmussen was born in Momence, Illinois, in October 1912, the son of a Baptist minister who moved his family west in the late 1930s. Wherever he went or whatever he did, Rasmussen was never afraid to try something new. He began a career as an aircraft mechanic for the Army Air Corps and in 1936 was hired by Lockheed Aircraft to oversee engine installations in P-38 fighters.

A passionate outsdoorman, Rasmussen missed country life. Near the end of World War II he decided to leave Southern California for Angel's Camp in Calaveras County where he started a lumber business. In the course of a few years his operation progressed from a small portable sawmill to established lumber mills in San Andreas and Chinese Camp near Jamestown in Tuolumne County.

"He developed a portable sawmill on wheels. He built all his own parts and could fix anything," says Clayton, Rasmussen's youngest son who quit his job as a forklift operator in 1967 to become one of Bear Valley's first employees. "He didn't have a college education, but he had a knowledge of how to build something from the ground up."

Rasmussen had little knowledge of the ski industry. He'd only learned to ski alongside his three sons and daughter at Dodge Ridge in the early 1950s, but he had a healthy respect for the mountains, a great love for sports in general and a strong knowledge of the outdoors. In what would become one of the longest preliminary planning periods in the history of ski resorts, Rasmussen took a leading role. He began by touring the area on skis and by snowcat, completing surveys of terrain and snow depth.

With an annual average snowfall of 360 inches, too little snow was not a problem. Near Ebbetts Pass 100 miles east of Stockton, the resort's base elevation begins at 6,400 feet and rises to 8,500 feet. From Mount Reba's ridge, the area is roughly divided into a north-facing and western bowl. From the top of the ski area Rasmussen discovered sweeping vistas of the Mokelumne River Valley, the volcanic Dardenelles and the Carson-Iceberg Wilderness. To the west he viewed the Hamilton Range and the lush, rolling countryside of the Mother Lode.

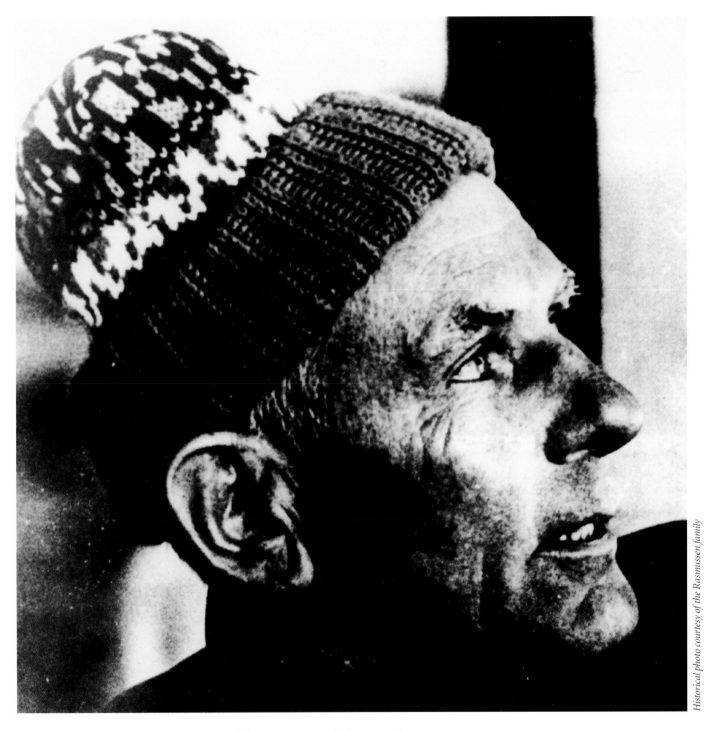

Historical photo courtesy of the Rasmussen family

"He was an extremely honest and generous man.
He wasn't one to be in the limelight, but he put his heart and soul into his community.
Many people today continue to enjoy the benefits from his dedication to Bear Valley," says son, Dennis.

In 1966 the U.S. Forest Service finally granted approval and the initial phase of development got underway with plans of opening the next year. Because of a late winter and deep snow pack, however, access to the area was impossible until well into the summer. "Close to 15 feet of snow fell in April," remembers Clayton. "We couldn't break ground until August."

Nonplussed, Rasmussen guided operations to rough out a nearly two mile access road to the newly reconstructed Highway 4. He cleared the parking lot area and oversaw construction of a $250,000 base lodge.

"It was an exciting time," says Clayton. "We were in on the ground level creating something new. It was amazing how quickly things started to take shape. He really pushed hard to get it done, and it got done."

The resort, first known as Mount Reba, opened for business in December 1967 to 600 skiers. By the end of the season weekend crowds averaged 4,500 skiers. Within a year the resort had firmly established itself by hosting the 1969 U.S. National Ski Championships. In the following years, with Rasmussen at the helm as general manager and vice president, Bear Valley continued to expand its facilities, even opening a Club Med hotel in its village.

"Maury managed by example. He was the kind of guy to whom everybody was equal," says Clayton who is Bear Valley's mountain manager. "He was the first person to jump into a situation even if it was hazardous. He went out on the mountain quite often to see how things were doing. He didn't sit in his office."

Rasmussen continued to be active in his community. He served as president of the Chamber of Commerce, the National Lumberman's Association and the Sierra Ski Operators Association. His passion for the ski business was equal to his passion for flying. He was directly responsible for founding the San Andreas Airport in 1954, was chairman of the Calaveras County Airport and was an active member of the Calaveras Flying Club and Experimental Aircraft Association of California. He even built his own Midget Mustang airplane on the front porch of his home in Bear Valley.

Rasmussen died of a heart attack in 1978 while working on a chairlift. "He'd been thinking of retirement, but he loved the mountains and he loved the business. It's where he wanted to be," says Dennis Rasmussen.

Courtesy of the Rasmussen family

It wasn't unusual for Maury to delight skiers at Bear Valley with aerial acrobatics on Sunday afternoons.

GREAT TEACHERS

© Tom Lippert

L U G G I

F O E G E R

—

B A D G E R   P A S S

A L P I N E

M E A D O W S

S K I   I N C L I N E

1907 – 1994

"Skiing is fun,"
he wrote in 1941.
"There is fun to be had
in the snow.
But it is more fun when it is
done correctly, skillfully
and safely."

uggi Foeger did not coin the phrase "Skiing is not just sport. It is a way of life!" The saying nonetheless captures the essence of America's Pied Piper of skiing. His talents and love for the sport created a life full of achievements, whether it be influencing a cadre of ski schools and instructors, as a soldier in wartime with the Tenth Mountain Division, as a professional photographer and cinematographer, or as a ski resort manager and developer.

"Luggi was always ahead of his time," explains Helen Foeger, his wife of forty-two years. "He was very outgoing and a lot of fun, but he was also very precise with organization and his method of ski school instruction."

He had been a top assistant at Hannes Schneider's ski school in St. Anton, Austria for ten years when he first met Don and Mary Tresidder from Yosemite Park & Curry Company in the mid-1930s. "They said, 'Luggi, if you ever have any ideas about leaving the country, come and see us.' And I didn't forget that." Foeger left Austria and went to New York and then Canada to consult on new ski areas at Banff and Lake Louise.

However, it wasn't long before his memory of the photographs of Yosemite in his school textbooks and the kind invitation from the Tresidders drew him to California and the ski school at Badger Pass.

The ski school flourished under Foeger's reorganization. At first, he found American ski students to be "impetuous, impulsive, and impatient," yet he soon discovered other qualities: that they were "always anxious to get ahead, and that they actually do learn much faster in their enthusiasm." Breaking away some from Schneider's formula, Foeger adapted the Arlberg technique into a more fluid motion. As he wrote in the Yosemite Winter Club Book in 1940, "The old system where a snowplow, a stem turn and a stem christiania are designated as three separate entities always seemed to me a very sad thing. The three turns should be built one on top of the other, and the perfect whole is the stem christiania."

Foeger not only had a gift for tutoring cautious and overanxious beginners into fine skiers, his engaging personality and reputation allowed him to recruit a milieu of top instructors into his ski school. Molding their skills into his philosophy, these disciples of his gospel continued to add a lustre to Badger Pass even after he moved on.

After the war, in which he and a handful of other famed skiers trained Tenth Mountain Division troops in skiing and winter survival, Foeger spent his winters at the Gray Rocks Inn in the Laurentians of Canada. He commented once, "In Canada it was hard to teach because it was so cold. We had to take crowbars to get through the ice to put slalom poles in. When we had a little snow, sometimes we wetted it so that the flag would stand up. You have to lace your boots indoors before they get so frozen and stiff that you can't pull them together." This situation encouraged him to return to Badger Pass in 1948 with a corps of young Canadian ski instructors, including Jim McConkey, Ross Moore, Claude LaChance and Nic Fiore. "Everybody wondered because they were

His goal was "to teach people how to ski with ease and grace."

Historical photo courtesy of Alpine Meadows

the least skiers there, but they had the best personalities for my suiting," Foeger said in a 1984 interview. "I said, personality is much more important than skiing. It's not a question of how fast you ski, it's a question of how accommodating you ski for your pupil."

"My ambition in life was to work for Luggi," admits Fiore, the Badger Pass ski school director since Foeger's departure in 1957. "He commanded a lot of respect but was entrenched in his methods. I learned this pretty quick. One year we were carrying a lot of camera gear skiing up to the Ostrander Hut where Luggi was making a movie called *Ski Thrills*, and shot entirely at Ostrander. We'd leave at daybreak, then start shooting. It was very intense. Luggi didn't like reshooting. I made the mistake of passing Luggi who was always the leader. This was a real no-no. Luggi was a stern disciplinarian. Everything had to be exact, and even though I was in awe, I'd just had the urge to pass him. The next day, he hands me my pack, and it felt pretty heavy, but he just explained that it was all camera equipment. When I finally got there I discovered he'd added 20 pounds of rocks!"

For all his recognition and precision, Foeger also enjoyed socializing and having fun. "He was always a comical guy," recalls Bill Klein who was best man at Foeger's wedding to Helen. "He would put on a wig and enter the room, or put onion rings over his ears at a dinner party. He could be really outgoing and jovial, just a wonderful person."

After leaving Yosemite, Foeger would head ski schools at Sugar Bowl and Alpine Meadows. He helped design Northstar-at-Tahoe and Ski Incline, where as its general manager he installed the first snowmaking in the Sierra Nevada. "It was very exciting to hear him talk about laying out a resort so it would be beneficial for people new to the sport," remembers his wife Helen, "He wasn't as interested in advanced skiers wanting to find new challenges. He worked more to develop skiers and design runs that everybody could enjoy. He did a wonderful job."

A man of many talents, he also developed the first modern-day safety binding and fit in a career as a photographer for the War Department where he worked on the ultra secret x-15 surveillance plane. Foeger was a man of multiple roles, but bringing people to the ski slopes remained a motivating force in his life.

His ambition to be the best was obvious in his work and play. He once said, "In Colorado, you have that fine powder. In Yosemite, you have that fantastic cement. Two days after it snowed when it was beautiful powder, it was hell. Cement was mostly the expression. I love that kind of stuff, because nobody else could ski it but me."

Luggi, sitting on the weasel, with Badger Pass skiers on a visit to Ostrander Hut.

oft-spoken and modest except when flying through buckle deep powder, Stan Tomlinson admits that it wasn't the Sierra Nevada that lured him to Squaw Valley in 1949 as much as famed French skier Emile Allais. "To me, Emile was the greatest skier in the world. He was a fantastic guy and I really wanted to learn from him."

When he discovered Allais was leaving Sun Valley to open up the ski school at a brand new ski resort in the West, Tomlinson asked if he could come along. "I'd been working as a ski patrolman, but Emile allowed me into the ski school."

It was the start of an association with Squaw Valley that lasted close to fifty years. Born in Vancouver, British Columbia, in 1924, Tomlinson was handed his first pair of skis of Peterborough ash when he was seven. His first memories are of skiing underneath the street lights of North Vancouver. Soon, he discovered the mountains held greater attractions.

"My brother was eleven years older and had started skiing before me. When I was old enough, I'd climb nearby Grouse Mountain with him. It was a long climb, over two hours, but I just remember I liked skiing down, although I didn't really know what I was doing."

By age fifteen he was ski racing on the weekends, mostly in a junior league, but that didn't stop him from capturing the Vancouver City Championships. "I seemed to pick it up right off the bat. I just loved to ski from the start. I really never wanted to do anything else."

A pilot in the Royal Canadian Air Force during World War II, Tomlinson headed back into the mountains after the war. "Military life wasn't nearly as much fun as skiing. As soon as I was discharged in 1946, I headed for a race at Steven's Pass in Washington. I never really went back to Canada."

Instead, he raced for Boise State in Idaho for a semester, then worked on ski patrol for Nelson Bennett at Sun Valley. He arrived at Squaw Valley a month before the resort opened in November 1949. "There were only six instructors that first year. It was a small area then with only one lift, but the chair was close to two miles long." Squaw Valley offered a variety of challenging runs and deep powder snow that lasted for weeks. He loved the spring skiing, and the weather wasn't as cold as in Idaho. Tomlinson decided to stick around.

Under Allais' tutelage, he learned the French parallel method. "It was based on sideslipping toward a parallel turn rather than the stem christie. Emile insisted on sideslipping to learn about edging. He never said a whole lot. He'd pick out one essential thing and work on it."

In 1951 Tomlinson spent a summer in Chile where he taught for Allais and worked at perfecting the heel kick and rotation of Allais' "rouade," or parallel turn. That same year, when Allais went to Europe to coach the U.S. Olympic Team, Tomlinson took over as the Squaw Valley ski school director and ran the program, on and off, into the 1970s.

S T A N
T O M L I N S O N
~
S Q U A W
V A L L E Y

*"Ski bums don't work.
I made my living skiing.
I just knew what I wanted
to do all along.
I wanted to live
in the mountains.
I wanted to be
a ski teacher and to ski.
I never pressured myself
to do anything else."*

© Carolyn Caddes

Even though he's more than seventy, Tomlinson still instructs an occasional private lesson each winter.
He tries to ski every day and in summer he rides his bike into the mountains
or plays a fast game of tennis with friends.

"I used what Emile taught me. I never thought one should talk much, that people learned by doing, not listening. A key to my success, however, was being able to demonstrate at a slow speed exactly what I wanted someone to do."

One person Tomlinson fondly recalls instructing through the years was entertainer Gene Kelly whom he first met in 1954. "He was a great athlete. He'd been a figure skater before a dancer so he adapted quickly to the snow. To tell the truth, what I most remember is his being bald. He never wore his hairpiece on the slopes so people wouldn't recognize him, much to his delight. He was a real gentleman, a pleasure to be around."

Though the French method was eventually abandoned with the advent of modern technical instruction, Tomlinson still acknowledges Allais' influence.

"New equipment and such has really helped teach people how to ski. You don't have these heavy boards anymore that you need to rotate. People talk of the old days, but all I remember about them is heavy, wet, cold feet. However, some things don't change. Emile had this infectious enthusiasm, and I think to be an instructor today you have to love to ski. You have to have a lot of enthusiasm every day you are out there."

Tomlinson's enthusiasm for the sport has made an impact on several generations of skiers. "Being trained by Stan on how to teach people to ski was one of the best things ever to happen to me," says Dick Dorworth, former director of the Aspen Ski School and coach of the U.S. Ski Team. "Stan taught me most of all that the ski profession was okay to get into and stay. He has always been an inspiration."

Stan Tomlinson and Pierre Gilbert skiing Headwall in the 1950s.

WERNER

SCHUSTER

—

ALPINE

MEADOWS

*"In 1967 when I took over
the Alpine Meadows' ski school,
I received a clipping
from my mother.
It read 'Make your business
be your hobby and
your hobby your business.'
Until then I'd always thought
of skiing as my great hobby.
All of a sudden I realized
how far into it I was.
I had indeed chosen to make
my hobby my business.
My heart was in teaching."*

lthough skiing was the focus of Werner Schuster's energetic life since he was a child growing up in Bavaria, it wasn't until many years later that he discovered just how much the sport meant to him.

The son of a merchant who sold ski equipment, Schuster grew up in the town of Immenstadt im Allgäu close to the Austrian and Swiss borders in Bavaria. As a teenager, he set the tone for his future, teaching ski customers who frequented his family's sporting goods store. "Just like today with many skiers, instructing was simply a way to finance my own skiing."

"I moved to Munich to work in my uncle's sports store. I missed the mountains. I was curious. I really wanted to go to a different country where there was a different language." His sense of adventure and exploratory spirit led him to Canada in 1958.

He landed a job teaching private school students to ski at Mont Royale in the heart of Montréal. Then he traveled north into the Laurentian Mountains to the town of Sainte Jovite where he found work at the popular Gray Rocks resort. Pleasant and gracious, with a sanguine manner that integrated his casual heart and soul attitude of mountain life with professionalism and savvy, Schuster immersed himself into the ski school, becoming one of the resort's most admired instructors.

"Gray Rocks was the resort that came up originally with the concept of the 'ski week' which they developed into an absolute art. I taught two seasons and became very familiar with the running of a ski school."

It was in Québec that Schuster's talent and timing coincided with meeting a fellow instructor from San Francisco. "My friend skied at Alpine Meadows and knew Luggi Foeger. He told me that Luggi was looking for an assistant for his ski school."

Schuster had never heard of Alpine Meadows or the Sierra Nevada. "I thought it was the same range as the Rockies." He certainly knew about Luggi Foeger, however, and jumped at the opportunity to work for the legendary skier. After a bit of correspondence expressing his interest, Schuster's formal agreement of employment handwritten by Luggi Foeger arrived in the form of a postcard. "I knew working for Luggi would be a great experience. Already, my vision was to one day run a ski school."

Schuster arrived at Alpine Meadows in December 1963, intending to stay for only one season. Thirty years later he still remembers his first impressions. "The mountains weren't spectacular like the Canadian Rockies, but the climate, all the nice sunny days and the abundance of snow were fabulous. After the cold of the Laurentians, it was like skiing in Hawaii. The longer I stayed the more I liked it."

Lured by its seductive landscape, he returned for another season and never left. He married his German girlfriend Hanni in 1965 and settled permanently in the Tahoe area to raise his family. Once again, he immersed himself in his job.

© Carolyn Caddes

"I'm involved in the business side of skiing now, but I never forget what we're selling.
It's not just a lift ticket, but an experience, an emotional experience, a family experience."

Studying his ski mentor's methods, Schuster was prepared to take over the ski school when Foeger departed Alpine Meadows in 1967. "I learned a lot from Luggi. He was demanding, yes. He dictated how he wanted to have his students taught, and you didn't question his authority. But he was a real mountain guy, and his enthusiasm, his love for the mountains and skiing really rubbed off."

Schuster had his own ideas, too. They leaned toward the business end of the sport and the marketing of a ski area. "I'd been impressed with the ski week idea at Gray Rocks. Even in Germany you taught the same students each weekend through the ski season. It led to a great amount of consistency and communication. American skiers were very demanding, in the sense that they expected to learn quickly. They wanted to see some progress. The ski week was perfect for that. My first year I began marketing weekly ski packages, hosting small groups out of the Bay Area."

Schuster also saw the need for a stronger standardization of ski instruction. "Because of Luggi, we taught the Austrian method. Next door at Squaw Valley, they taught the French method. If you traveled to Mammoth, Max Goode taught the Swiss style. It didn't make any sense. Students needed to get the same message, no matter where they went."

Schuster pushed for better teaching standards. After earning his own certification, he became an examiner and then was elected president of the Western chapter of the Professional Ski Instructors of America. In 1975 he was elected president of the national organization.

Marketing strategies continued to taunt him with a clear view of what ski resorts needed to attract increasing numbers of skiers to the slopes. "Most resorts didn't have a marketing department. It was the ski school director who was the spokesperson for the resort and the promotional arm for the ski area. He was the expert on the skiing, the weather and the mountain."

Under Schuster's guidance, Alpine Meadows developed marketing schemes that attracted ski clubs and schools. Schuster's input became so influential it eventually drew him away from his ski school and into full-time marketing responsibilities. When he left his position as ski school director in 1978, his staff had grown from six people to more than 120 instructors teaching 30,000 skiers a season.

"It was tough leaving the outdoor side of the sport. Just the personal contacts I made over those years, with students as well as instructors, were very rewarding. But economics dictated where my career could grow."

Schuster's role at Alpine Meadows even outgrew a marketing capacity. Today he is the resort's vice president, involved in product analysis, new business potential, and corporate acquisitions. In 1996 Schuster's outstanding contributions to skiing were recognized by the North American Ski Journalists Association when he was given the Charley Proctor Award.

"I'm involved in the business side of skiing now, but I never forget what we're selling. It's not just a lift ticket, but an experience, an emotional experience, a family experience. If you can get that message across to people who have never even experienced snowsport, then skiing will always have a competitive advantage over other choices of recreation. It is truly a lifestyle we can sell sincerely because it's the one we've opted for."

Courtesy of Alpine Meadows

Werner Schuster carving an elegant turn.

"People treat me as
professionally as anyone else.
Being a ski instructor
is a small living,
but a respectable living.
To be active in the mountains,
enjoying the water, the snow,
the dusty roads with the dogs,
you bet it's a good life."

ne of the few regrets Babette Haueisen has about her skiing career is that she didn't discover teaching sooner. "I'd always been a ski racer. Then I broke a leg and an ankle in 1956 and the racing career ended."

Traveling to Europe the next year after her recovery, Haueisen was introduced to an Austrian ski instructor. He invited her to attend a ski instructor's college in St. Christophe. "That was my professional introduction. Next thing I knew I was in St. Anton teaching. It was wonderful. I was no longer a ski bum! I felt like I fit. This was my niche."

A native of Wisconsin, Haueisen didn't put on her first pair of skis until she was nineteen and a student at Marin Junior College in San Francisco's North Bay in 1949. She joined the Berkeley Ski Club in 1952, but skiing on the weekends wasn't enough, so she moved to Donner Summit to work as a ticket checker at Sugar Bowl. The pay was only $150 a month, but it included room and board. "Bill Klein took me under his wing and I got to ski with the Austrian boys. Bill would always tell everybody 'She goes fast between falls.'" Her ability progressed so rapidly that within a ski season she was winning most of the races she entered. At Dodge Ridge, she won so many of the "Sunday Slalom" races that the resort finally picked up her entry fee.

While Haueisen has discovered her lifelong occupation, it was ski racing that formed the foundation for her career as a ski teacher. "Racing was so much fun, just competing. I loved the snow. My parents thought I was nuts. They'd tell me I couldn't stay in the mountains, I needed to find a job. I'd say to them 'I can look at my life and dream.'"

In 1955 she captured the prestigious Silver Belt at Sugar Bowl and the Roch Cup in Aspen. At the 1956 Olympic Trials in Stowe, Vermont, she placed in the top ten in the slalom, giant slalom, and downhill events, but still missed out on making the team. "I wore bib No. 1. Was I nervous! I remember Andrea Mead trying to get me to concentrate. 'Pump your rump!' she'd say."

Ski racing and coaching were satisfying, but it was her European experience that taught Haueisen the fine elements of ski instruction. "In Austria, I learned how an instructor is really the leader of a tour. You learn to handle anything that might happen on the mountain."

At the opening ceremonies of the 1960 Winter Olympic Games, Haueisen was chosen to ski into Squaw Valley on barrel staves and relay the Olympic torch to Starr Walton. The next year, with the opening of Alpine Meadows, she asked a less-than-enthusiastic Luggi Foeger for a job in his ski school. "There were five men and no women instructors. Luggi was old school. He told me he didn't need a woman in his ski school, but I was determined. I kept hanging around until he finally hired me as part of the staff."

© Carolyn Caddes

Babette in her 1967 Mercedes 240SL. "I was in San Francisco in 1977 and saw this car in the window.
I asked the salesman to hold it for me. I went home and mortgaged my house to buy it."

Working under Alpine Meadows' next ski school director, Werner Schuster, she became fully certified in 1963 and taught at Alpine Meadows for sixteen years.

After a short stint as head of the ski school at Soda Springs, she moved to Northstar-at-Tahoe in 1982 where she has taught ever since. Of 150 instructors, Haueisen continues to be requested by patrons more than any other.

In 1995 Haueisen was named as one of the "Top One Hundred" ski instructors in the nation by *Skiing* magazine. She was selected, not just for her technical excellence, but her ability to facilitate skill development and teach a class or private lesson with equal success. Haueisen is one of ten instructors in the Sierra Nevada to receive the recognition.

"Being named to the list was certainly a pinnacle of my instructing career. I think a lot of my success has come from taking a personal interest in my students. I learn their names. I try to put myself into the athletic ability of the people I'm teaching. When there is personal involvement, the student will do his best to try and do what you're teaching. I want to see a skier born every second."

"My motto is
'Come Ski With Miss B.'
Whether they are seniors
or entry level,
I still enjoy teaching and
will enjoy it forever.
The rewards of making
people into skiers are
what keep me out there
day after day.
After all these years
I've taught four generations
of skiers, including
my third generation of twins."

Photo by Tom Lippert, courtesy of Northstar-at-Tahoe

Courtesy of Babette Haueisen

Babette admits that she loved going fast. Here she is in racing form, heading for the finish line.

*"The old Arlberg technique
was a simple way to ski.
All I did was cut down,
do more leg work and
stay square over the skis.
I had a lot of people here
support me about
the way I teach."*

t seventy-five, Gus Weber looks more like an ex-rodeo cowboy than a ski instructor, hands gnarled, legs bowed and back bent. It's almost hard to imagine him on skis, but, then again, his eyes are sparkling, and a smile comes easily to his craggy, furrowed face. This is a mountain man who has thrived on fresh air, winter winds and the exhilaration of a downhill ride.

He was born in Zug, Switzerland, in 1921, and skied well enough to race on the Swiss Team and teach skiing. But it wasn't enough. Gustav Weber wanted to see more of the world, an ambition he says he inherited from his grandfather, a train engineer who worked on the Blue Train in South Africa. He says a teacher once told him, "You don't know very much, but you're sure good in geography."

He came by boat to Canada in 1951. By trade, Weber was a staircase builder. "When I came over here, I looked around, and I see all the houses we got here don't need a stairway, they only need a few steps. I realized the only way I could make a go of it would be to go to them old cities with fancy homes and replace the old stairways. That would have been all right, but I always got kinda homesick for the mountains, so I decided to forget it."

Drawn to the mountains, he went to Mont Tremblant in the Laurentians to teach skiing. He stayed for three years and met other "famous hell-raisers" like Jim McConkey and Ernie McCullough. Weber liked Canada and the Canadians, but not the cold. "After 25 below, they didn't turn on the lifts." He traveled west, as so many of his colleagues from Mont Tremblant had done. During one winter season while teaching skiing at Snow King in Jackson, Wyoming, he heard about Dave McCoy and Mammoth Mountain which was about to open with its first chairlift.

Weber wrote to McCoy about a job and then went to see him on Thanksgiving 1955, the ski area's opening day. At thirty-four, he still wasn't certain about his future. "In Switzerland if you're a ski instructor, it's like being a professor in high school or college, but here you're a ski bum." But when Dave McCoy offered him a job to run the Mammoth ski school, Weber knew he had found a home and a place to advance his own method of teaching.

Weber based his skiing technique on what he learned from ski racing. "You stay over the skis and keep your natural position." The popular method of teaching at that time was Kruckenhauser's Austrian technique. "I couldn't stand it—the reverse shoulder technique. Anytime you do this, you tighten up. The leg action is already shot, the edge control stiffens up. So, why not ski the way you walk?"

During his first summer at Mammoth, Weber found another passion when he bought a horse and a mule. He would spend his summers packing into the Eastern Sierra backcountry to clear hiking trails and carry supplies. "That was the smartest thing I did. You're by yourself and nothing around, no telephone, no cars, just you and the stock and a dog or two. Then I got time to think about life. In the ski business, you can go belly-up in a hurry, just partying, partying and pretty soon, it becomes a way of life."

© Tom Lippert

Gus Weber and his horse Rebel on a ranch near Bishop, California. Born Gustav and nicknamed "Gusti" in Switzerland,
he's not sure he likes the shortened version of his name given to him by Americans.
"The only thing is, every pack station has a mule by the name of Gus. Even the Walt Disney mule is named Gus."

The new national ski instructors' association didn't approve of Weber's ski technique despite his skill at skiing any snow condition with style. "When I came here, there was nobody who could ski breakable snow with ice on top. I was all by myself. If you're by yourself, it's not much fun to go. Later on, I started to get some instructors out, too. You need the right technique. You have to get out of the snow. You have to go down, get up, you have to have good legs. That's why I always stress leg action and turn towards the fall line in the air, and when you break through, then again you have even weight on both skis, and you just finish the turn."

Although his teaching methods were successful with his students at Mammoth, the instructor's association wanted Weber to adapt to its standards and style. "I had a good reputation. That's what ticked me off. Some of those officials couldn't even keep up in our top class in ski school as a student." Weber's stubbornness and the association's unwillingness to bend caused a rift that wouldn't be repaired. "I quit. I just couldn't put up with something I don't believe in. If the other instructors had left me in the dust coming down the hill and proved to me that their thing was any better, it would have been easier."

After fifteen years as ski school director of Mammoth Mountain, the Swiss cowboy rode out of town. Gus Weber never married. "Nobody asked me." And decades of skiing, riding and hell-raising are taking their toll on this wrangler's body. "Everything starts to stiffen up. My mother had the same problem. She always worked hard. I never could understand. Now I'm finding out."

Gus Weber's other passion, the backcountry of the Eastern Sierra. Here is where he spent his summers, packing people in and sharing his love of these mountains.

© Ellie Huggins

© Ray Atkeson

Emile Allais, the great French skier and first director of the ski school at Squaw Valley, brought the French parallel technique to ski instruction, influencing a generation of instructors and racers.

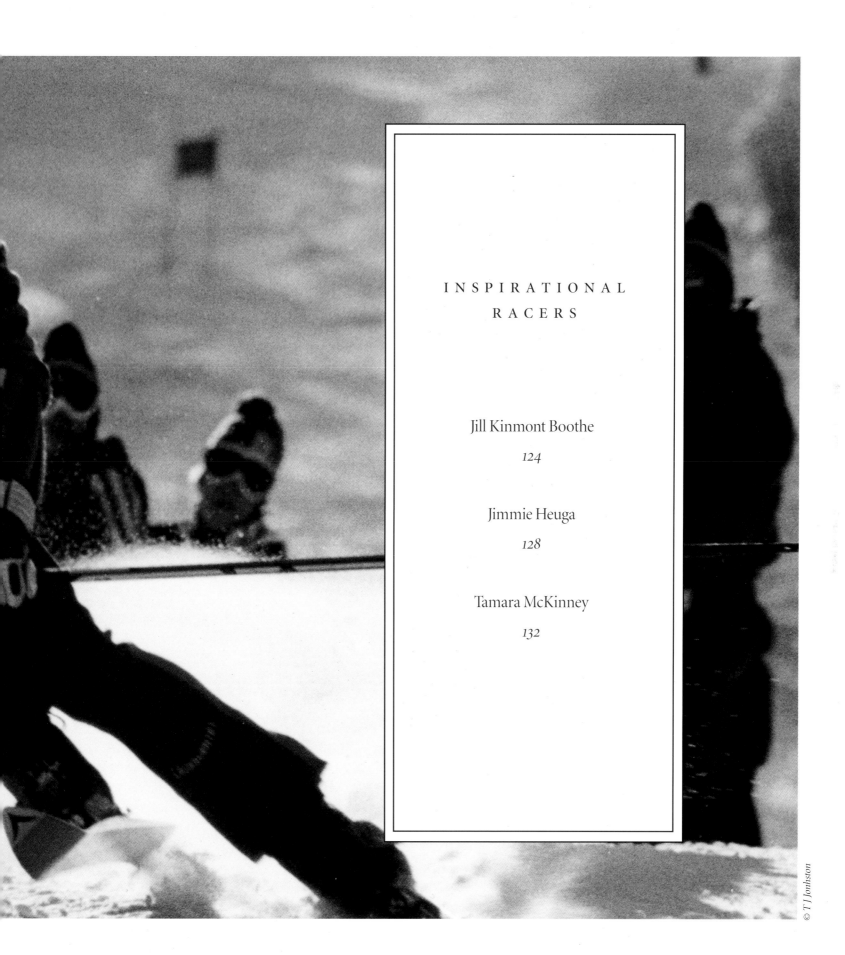

INSPIRATIONAL RACERS

The determination
that made her a ski champion
allowed her to resurrect
a life on her own terms,
and one that would break away
from the isolated world
of the handicapped.

I n February 1955, eighteen-year-old Jill Kinmont was riding the crest of a promising wave as she stood at the top of the race course listening carefully to Andrea Mead Lawrence, Olympic Gold Medalist and America's foremost woman skier. Kinmont was ready to make her run in the Snow Cup giant slalom at Alta, Utah, the first in a series of tryout races for the 1956 U.S. Olympic Ski Team.

Swift and sure on her skis, Kinmont, a Bishop, California, high school graduate, was one of America's prized Olympic ski prospects from Dave McCoy's stable of talented Mammoth Ski Club racers. The snub-nosed, pretty blonde skier, who once thought herself so skinny that she ate ice cream sundaes every day after school to gain weight, had startled the world of ski racing the season before by becoming the only woman ever to win the National Junior and Senior Slalom in the same year. In addition, she won a second gold medal as National Open Slalom Champion beating all professional skiers in the race as well as amateurs. In all, her achievements that year earned her the Andrea Mead Lawrence Award, honoring her as America's outstanding junior woman skier, and an invitation to Christian Pravda's national team training camp in Sun Valley.

A young lady of homespun values, Kinmont had grown up on her dad's alfalfa farm in the Owens Valley near Mammoth, which doubled as the Rocking K Guest Ranch for skiers and fly fishermen.

Dave McCoy, her race coach and mentor, was a strong influence in all aspects of her life. "He had the greatest attitude towards life. If you worked hard towards something, you could succeed. It didn't matter what it was. Even if your self-esteem was lacking, he had a way of proving you could do it, but at the same time making you demonstrate to yourself you could do it." McCoy instilled in Kinmont the belief that winners never made little mistakes. They were never lazy for a tenth of a second, and they had a fast finish on every turn.

Kinmont's racing results impressed major magazines such as *Life* and *Sports Illustrated*. When interviewed, she'd charm reporters with a swooning grassroots effervescence, explaining that she skied simply because "it's so much fun."

At Alta, Kinmont did as always, and pushed herself to the limit. Her following run and resulting mistakes would change her life forever.

Entering a steep gully known as The Corkscrew, with a treacherous wind at her back, Kinmont sped too fast on her Kneissel Kanonens to prejump its four-foot knoll. Flung into wild, uncontrolled flight, she slammed into a spectator then cartwheeled into a tree. In the middle of her final tumble she felt a sudden dull vibration. Then she felt nothing. She lay in the snow, moaning, "My God, what have I done?"

Later, it would be said that she had been ahead of everyone by ten seconds when she crashed. Only the week before she'd been on the cover of *Sports Illustrated*. Now, within a few seconds, her life lay shattered. Her spinal cord was completely severed low in the neck, causing permanent

© Carolyn Caddes

After thirty years of teaching, specializing in learning disorders, Jill Kinmont retired in the spring of 1996
to her home and husband in Bishop. She lives not far from the ranch where she grew up
and her paintings show her love of the changing light on the landscapes of the eastern Sierra and the high desert around Bishop.

paralysis, both motor and sensory, below the shoulder. Doctors were more concerned with whether Kinmont would live than whether she would ever ski again.

But survive she did. Blessed with a quiet determination and a cool grasp of reality, Kinmont did more than merely persevere.

Once stabilized she began an incredible odyssey, full of more obstacles than a slalom course, but one which would bring her worldwide admiration. At first, she felt robbed. She was also bored. Sometimes she'd count the dots on the speckled ceiling of her hospital room—there were 8,192 she claimed. What she missed most was feeling: the brush of tall grass against her legs and the satin touch of a horse's nose.

She also learned how to win again. She didn't mind using a wheelchair, but she didn't intend to look as if she belonged in one. During her race career, her physical training program at her father's guest ranch included an appalling dose of self-discipline. So, too, did her rehabilitation. Luckily, her breathing remained unimpaired and her arms retained some function. At the California Rehabilitation Center in Los Angeles she exercised with weights and pulleys. She learned to feed herself, push her own wheelchair, paint and write. Outside, the apple blossoms came and went, the locust trees bloomed, the lilacs arrived then faded, and by 1957, the girl who'd learn to ski slalom around stripped willow stalks Dave McCoy had cut along the banks of the Owens River wheeled herself onto the UCLA campus to enroll for college classes.

She graduated in 1961 with a bachelor of arts degree in German and a scholarship to the University of Vienna. Returning from Europe, she registered for several postgraduate courses in education but was denied entrance to universities because of her physical handicap. Kinmont relentlessly pursued her quest to become a teacher and eventually found acceptance at the small Clinic School at UCLA.

In 1963 the Kinmont family moved to Renton, Washington, a few miles east of Seattle. Jill entered the College of Education at the University of Washington, achieving credentials for both elementary and secondary education. As a student teacher at the Ingraham School in Seattle she taught four classes a day. Her success astounded critics and helped shed the image that the disabled could not compete or contribute in everyday life. She continued her teaching in Los Angeles but eventually was drawn back to her hometown of Bishop. She started a summer school at the nearby Paiute Indian Reservation in Owens Valley and established the Jill Kinmont Indian Education Fund.

In 1967 the world of skiing claimed Kinmont forever as one of their own by voting her into the U.S. National Ski Hall of Fame. A Hollywood motion picture about her life called The Other Side of the Mountain *and two biographies followed.*

Jill Kinmont in 1953. Two years later she became the only woman to win both the junior and senior women's slalom title in the same year.

"The mountains gave me strength, the chance to get back on the slopes, to do things with my friends, to have snow blow in my face. When skiing I no longer felt sorry for myself."

A s the 1964 Winter Olympic Games in Innsbruck, Austria, came to a close, Americans were becoming concerned with the total medal shutout of the United States men's alpine ski team. However, on the next to last day of the Games, American men finally made a historic breakthrough.

Starting out of the second seed, twenty-year-old Jimmie Heuga, without goggles or a hat, quickly negotiated the bone-hard Patscherkofel course. Gaining momentum, he zipped into the final tight combinations of the steilhang. "My concentration was so incredible that I remember being aware of the announcer over the speakers telling the crowd the time I needed to win. I was so fired up. I kind of needed the distraction."

Undaunted, Heuga's second run propelled him solidly into third place, only a quarter second behind teammate Billy Kidd who missed the gold, won by Austrian "Pepi" Steigler, by only .14 of a second.

"To tell the truth, I was disappointed I'd gotten third. A video later shows me taking off my glove and throwing it at the ground in disgust."

Temporarily upset, Heuga took off his skis while the estimated crowd of 65,000 roared in disbelief. Kidd had won the silver, Heuga the bronze. Two American racers had triumphed for the first time in Olympic competition over the invincible Europeans.

"Everybody was stunned. Billy began punching me in the arm. Bob Beattie, our coach, was so excited he ran and stumbled down the side of the course from the start to reach us in the finish corral. He was in shock."

That night, Heuga entered Innsbruck's Aufsprungbahn arena for the medal ceremony. As the Olympic torch glowed and mountain bugles played, the overflow of spectators sprawled up the dark mountainside toward the Brenner Pass.

"The night before we'd been shoved around by this security guard. Now he was ushering me to the victory stand. The crowd was fantastic. It was a really exciting moment."

A week after the Olympics, Heuga won the slalom at the prestigious Arlberg-Kandahar in Garmisch, Germany, a win that has yet to be duplicated by an American. Heuga continued to create respect for U.S. racers. In 1966 he finished fourth in the combined at the World Championships in Portillo, Chile. The following year he skied to third place overall in World Cup giant slalom competition. In 1968 he graced the cover of *Sports Illustrated* and had two top ten finishes at the Winter Olympics in Grenoble, France. All in all, he spent ten years on the U.S. National team, competed in two World Championships and in two Olympics, and won two national ski titles.

"It was a neat thing, us doing so well, and it had a lot of impact in Europe. The team I was part of was an amazing group. Buddy Werner was the oldest by far and his best year had probably been 1959, but he was a great leader. There was a sense of cohesiveness and sacrifice among us. Bob Beattie had this inspirational knack for putting us on the threshold."

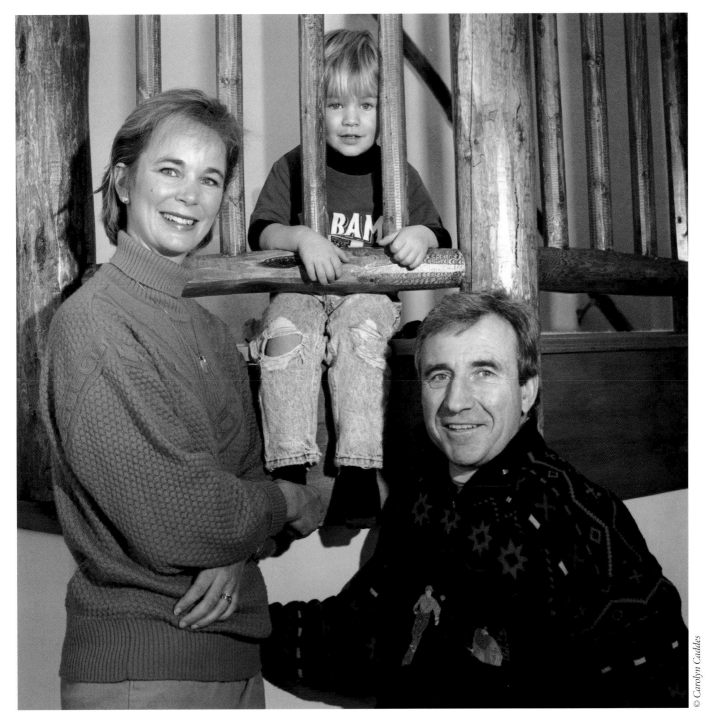

© Carolyn Caddes

Jimmie and Debbie with their youngest son Winston. "The main thing is never to give up on yourself. Take each day one at a time. I'm always getting knocked on my butt, but I've decided to live out my life. My life exists ahead of me, not in the past."

Born in San Francisco in 1943 to French-Basque parents, Heuga moved with his family to Lake Tahoe at age two. When his father, Pascal, went to work for Squaw Valley in 1949, Heuga grew up skiing on one of North America's great ski mountains.

"Emile Allais, who was the Squaw Valley ski school director, took me under his wing. He also coached the national team and he'd invite top racers like Brooks Dodge, Ralph Miller and Buddy Werner to train at Squaw. I was really young but got to ski with all these great people. Emile taught me the joy and fun of ski racing. I've never forgotten it. He taught me to always enjoy what you're doing."

In 1958 Heuga met racing coach Willi Schaeffler. In his 22 years as the coach at Denver University, German-born Schaeffler and his teams won fourteen National Collegiate titles and 100 out of 123 dual meets.

"Willi was a pretty strict guy, but he really helped me. More than technique, however, he taught me how to take responsibility for my own actions. Even if it was a lousy weather day, or things weren't going right, he would say 'You can take any day and make it a good day.' His favorite expression was 'Come to attention,' which, interpreted, meant to create your own circumstances."

Heuga needed such lessons in life. During the 1968 Olympics, Heuga's timing appeared off. He felt sluggish. "I thought it was burnout." But numbness, blurry vision, and a feeling of being emotionally flat lingered. In 1970, a spinal tap confirmed his doctor's suspicions. Heuga was diagnosed with multiple sclerosis, a neurological disabling disease with no known cure.

For the next several years his energy steadily sank. He was forced to stop skiing altogether. It took all his strength to put his ski boots on, let alone ski down even the easiest of terrain. Doctors urged him to save his energy and avoid stress, or he'd end up on his back.

By 1972, as his conditioned worsened, Heuga passively watched the Winter Olympics in Sapporo, Japan, on television from his home in Connecticut. His marriage had ended. Two sports stores in which he had an interest were failing. He felt uncertain and unmotivated.

"There was no doubt I'd been feeling sorry for myself, but ski racing taught me about setting goals, having priorities. There are always setbacks, but not defeat. I drew a distinction between the disease and my health. I was determined not to watch my life pass before me."

He'd lost the ability to run, but he still had his English racing bike. "At first I couldn't get on it. I fell and fell and fell, but it didn't matter. The fatigue and sweat made me remember how good it felt to be alive."

Heuga resolved to take control of his life. He attacked his disease head on. Soon he was pedaling 25 miles a week and exercising daily. He moved back to the mountains and resumed skiing. He created a program of cardiovascular endurance, stretching and strengthening exercises. Doctors doubted his regimen but agreed that his exercising caused no sign of further damage.

Young Jimmie getting some air.

Courtesy of Carson White

By 1981 he began spreading his philosophy to others with multiple sclerosis. He spent the next three years working with the National Multiple Sclerosis Society, visiting and encouraging MS patients to regain self-esteem, to be active and to maximize their health.

"There's no mystery to this. There's nothing scientific. It kind of goes back to what Willi told me about taking command of your life. Problems can become a crutch and create handicaps beyond the disability, but life is what we make it. I went back and got myself off the ground. I had to stop skiing for awhile, but I went on to the things I could do. I set myself some realistic instead of futile goals and took it from there."

In 1984 Heuga established the Jimmie Heuga Center in Vail, Colorado, a non-profit scientific research organization "to reanimate the physically challenged. Reanimation means to bring back to life. This center is for people to regain a quality of life, to teach patients to challenge MS, to stay in as good condition as possible."

Heuga continues to challenge medical thinking, and his message continues to travel nationwide through annual ski and biking events. His center has grown to include satellite operations coast to coast. Heuga travels thousands of miles a year, fundraising and visiting those with ongoing medical programs.

"The things that were important are still important. Being in the mountains, on the hill. I'm so fortunate to have met the woman of my dreams, Debbie. I have three wonderful children. I know I can make a mark with this project."

Emile Allais, the great race teacher talks with two star pupils, Jimmie Heuga and Jean-Claude Killy, at an American Express race at Beaver Creek.

© Tom Lippert

*"The mountains and skiing
are my love.
They've been a strength for me."*

ew people were betting on Tamara McKinney to win a gold medal at the 1989 World Championships at Vail, Colorado. Swiss reigning champion Vreni Schneider had been dominant all season long. McKinney's best slalom finishes had been a second and two thirds, but she hadn't been able to put together a pair of winning runs in the same race all season long.

However, being the underdog didn't phase the woman that *Time* magazine called "America's Queen of the Hill." McKinney skied a magnificent opening run in the slalom, beating Schneider's first attempt by an apparently overwhelming margin of 1.17 seconds. But Schneider produced an explosive second run that shot her .12 second ahead of McKinney to win. Schneider now seemed destined for the combined gold even though neither she nor McKinney was an exceptional downhiller. Schneider had finished a surprising fifth in a World Cup downhill two seasons before. McKinney had never done anything close to that.

Schneider went down the Vail course in eighth position to keep her in first place overall. McKinney, racing from the 16th position, shrugged off the pressure of Schneider's result. Popping out of the gate she hit the course with a vengeance. Remembering the advice of her old race coach, Anderl Molterer, "to go like a Mother Goose," at the first interval her speed was better than Schneider's. A previously uninspired hometown crowd began to cheer, the sound increasing to a deafening roar. "I could actually hear them yelling through my helmet."

Riding that wave of support, McKinney beat Schneider by more than a second, giving the petite Squaw Valley resident the World Championship combined gold medal. At the press conference later, a reporter asked the Sierra Nevada native how she felt. McKinney paused for a moment, her eyes glistening with joy, and gave out an unbridled, "Yahoo!"

"When I got back to my hotel room after the press conference," she recalls, "there was a big bunch of roses with a simple note which said, 'You went like Mother Goose!'"

The youngest of seven brothers and sisters, McKinney came from a family of determination and athleticism. Her father, Rigan, was a famous steeplechase jockey, elected to the Horseracing Hall of Fame in 1968. Skiing was a family tradition; Tamara has a photograph of her grandmother soaring off the ski jump at Lake Placid in a skirt.

Her parents divorced when she was only five and her mother, Frances, a ski instructor at Mount Rose, raised the seven children, nurturing an extraordinary family of racers. McKinney's sister, Sheila, was in World Cup competition when she was twelve. Brother Steve, a U.S. Ski Team downhiller, broke five records in speed skiing and was the only alpinist to hang glide off Mount Everest.

Tamara was the youngest and by far the smallest of the children. She remembers when her mother put her in a little open suitcase which her siblings would tow while her mother taught skiing. "Steve would occasionally take me out of the suitcase and put me on his shoulders. He'd just take off down the mountain, screaming down a slope, holding me around his neck with one hand."

© Tom Lippert

Tamara McKinney with her World Cup trophies, and around her neck, a small medal, the first she ever won.
"I was pretty determined to do well. I kept reminding myself what Anderl Molterer, my old race coach, had drilled into me.
To go 'like a Mother Goose.'"

McKinney was coached by legendary skiers Anderl Molterer, Christian Pravda, Philipe Mollard and Tito Pardone. She skied her first World Cup at age fourteen. Two years later she climbed the World Cup trophy steps, finishing third in a World Cup slalom at Piancavallo, Italy.

McKinney won her first World Cup race in 1981 at age twenty-one. She was the first American woman to win an overall World Cup title in 1983. She won the World Cup giant slalom in 1981 and 1983 and the slalom title in 1984. She captured World Championship bronze medals in 1985 and 1987, and gold and bronze in 1989. She also won nine national alpine titles, 18 World Cup races, and competed in three Olympics.

"Tamara always had tremendous feeling in her skis," noted U.S. women's ski coach Ernst Hager. McKinney explained it much simpler. "I've always had fun skiing. It's just my way of having a good time."

She even managed to smile through mistakes. After crashing into a Italian spectator when she was seventeen and breaking her arm, she said, "Just tell Mom I finally fell for an Italian."

She was also able to forget the bad races and focus on the good. In a 1985 interview she revealed, "When the skiing is there, it's like musicians when they have something in their head they translate into beautiful music—an expression of feeling. I can get technical and describe what the angles are and how they work, I know that. What I just need is that feeling, that freedom to let the beauty happen. You always have to be able to find something very positive, otherwise, it's really difficult to get through it."

Marvelous as her record was, her outlook on life also helped her endure disappointments and family tragedies. After she placed second in a World Cup giant slalom in 1985, she called home to share the good news and learned that her father had died, suffering a stroke that morning at age 77. In 1977 her sister Sheila crashed during a World Cup downhill and fell into a coma. She spent a year unable to walk or speak properly and never raced again. Both her brothers died in heart-breaking circumstances. She left her ailing mother's side to compete on a broken leg in the 1988 Calgary Olympics. A month later her mother died of cancer.

During her racing career she persevered through a succession of injuries, but the last, a fall at Saas-Fee, Switzerland, in 1989 broke her leg in ten places and forced her to retire from World Cup racing at age twenty-eight. What did survive through McKinney's roller coaster life was a strong spirit and love of the sport.

McKinney returned to ski racing on a professional level. In 1993 she won the overall Tournament of Champions, and she became a spokesperson for the Jimmie Heuga Foundation. Although she is taking time out from skiing, she dreams of organizing and coaching a junior race program for underfinanced youths in the Lake Tahoe area.

"When everything is coming down hard, skiing is my release, my freedom. More than anything, through these drastic changes in my life, I've learned how much I care and what certain people mean to me."

*"I learned a lot from Jimmie,
mainly to always get out and
do the best you can
with what you have.
It goes along with what
my mother once told me:
'Don't ever give up something
you care about because
of someone or something else.
You never will know
what you'll be able to do.'
To be skiing and helping people
at the same time, hey,
I feel pretty lucky."*

Tamara and Jimmie during a promotion for the Jimmie Heuga Express.

Above Alpine Meadows.

SAVING
THE VISION

—

ALPINE
MEADOWS

*Though the ski industry
has entered a new era
of consolidation and
corporate mergers,
Badami still believes that
passion and dreams,
not marketing surveys and
focus groups,
should continue
to shape its future.*

he only reason I've had success is because I have gray hair so people have listened to me." Nick Badami, chairman of U.S. Skiing and chief executive officer of Powdr Corporation, jokes about his accomplishments, which are as impressive as his energy. At seventy-six, he's still in control, overseeing the operation of four ski areas: Alpine Meadows, Boreal, and Soda Springs near Lake Tahoe and Park City in Utah.

Like many others who came to live, work and play in the mountains, Badami traveled a long distance to reach the Sierra Nevada. He admits that he was just looking for a hobby when he bought Alpine Meadows in 1970.

"The ski business appealed to me. Nobody was working in it to make a living. People worked for the love of the sport and the mountains. The competition among resorts wasn't for a share of the skier market, rather for a share of the recreation dollar. Also, it was a product nobody needed, but all the customers came because it was pure fun. Lastly, it was a business staffed by young, aggressive, intelligent people."

Badami's reputation and wealth had already been made in the garment industry as one of the principals of BVD apparel, a conglomerate of ten manufacturing divisions and two retail chains. "Technically I retired when I left BVD, but where else but in skiing can somebody my age associate with so many young people?"

He was an unlikely candidate for the sport which he now enthusiastically advocates. New York City-born, Badami attended the Wharton School of Finance at the University of Pennsylvania before honing his skills in the apparel business. He'd never even put on a pair of skis until 1969 when he was forty-eight. Nevertheless, he quickly established himself in the ski industry with his purchase of fledgling ski resorts headed toward bankruptcy, the first being Alpine Meadows in 1970. In his first year at the helm, the resort ended the season in the black, reversing a long history of annual losses.

"When I took over Alpine Meadows the only management person who left was the president. The resort had good people and a wonderful reputation with its customers. The problem wasn't in its operation; it was lacking in basic business principles. I had to become a teacher in business planning and control. It was as simple as that."

Badami shrugs off the pressures of operating a ski area. He explains that he leaves the mountain operations in the hands of experts while concentrating on what he knows best: policy, budgeting and acquisitions. "It's not a one-man deal. You have to have good middle and top management. My job is to plot the course."

Confident of his goals and high standards, Badami bought the fledgling Park City ski resort in 1975, also in financial trouble. He focused on putting the downhill experience before the uphill experience: investing in snowmaking before new lifts. His investment and business acumen rewarded him with a windfall after Park City became the headquarters for the U.S. Ski Team and

© Carolyn Caddes

"The ski business appealed to me.
Nobody was working in it to make a living.
People worked for the love of the sport and the mountains."

the site chosen for the alpine events at the 2002 Winter Olympic Games. Meanwhile, Alpine Meadows with its snowmaking capabilities successfully weathered snowless winters, even reporting banner years in the late 1980s when nearby resort operators suffered financial losses.

"People want value for their dollars; they want a quality experience and the ability to have fun. When you can have a consistent and stable product combined with a mature work force, then you have a product ready for the public. We're highly service-oriented. We're very sensitive to surrounding communities."

He displays a remarkable ease, with the air of a man enjoying himself. He has a way of making people feel at home, of belonging. It comes not so much from his success, but from the sport that he has embraced wholeheartedly. But, it hasn't always been smooth sailing. Badami's decade-long dream of constructing a destination ski resort atop Nevada's Mount Rose in the Galena drainage met with stringent bureaucratic and environmentally vocal opposition. After ten years of effort, he stopped the project and allowed a public buyout of his 3,684-acre dream by a national, nonprofit land conservation group.

Badami had already experienced far greater and deeper trials. On March 31, 1982, after a continuous Sierra storm had dumped close to 20 feet of snow on Alpine's upper slopes, a rogue avalanche swept away the bottom terminal building of the Summit chairlift and spread into the base lodge and parking lot, killing seven people. Less than a decade later, personal tragedy struck Badami in Park City when Craig, his only child, died at age 37 in a helicopter crash just after directing a successful World Cup event.

Many insiders felt that, after his son's death, Badami might retire at age seventy. Instead, he immersed himself even more in the ski industry. He served as chairman of the National Ski Areas Association from 1986 to 1988 and the American Ski Federation from 1988 to 1990. He continued to direct the Avalanche Foundation from 1987 until 1992 and became chairman of U.S. Skiing in 1995 after ten years as a board member. When the Powdr Corporation bought Alpine Meadows of Tahoe, Inc., the holding company for Alpine Meadows and Park City, in May 1994, he remained chairman of the board and chief executive officer for the new owners. The following year he helped expand Powdr Corporation's holding by leading the acquisition of Boreal and Soda Springs ski areas on Donner Summit.

Badami was awarded the National Ski Areas Association Lifetime Achievement Award, a tribute to a man who has demonstrated an extraordinary commitment to the ski industry.

"The ski business has become more sophisticated, yet it is still a fun business. The industry is trying to veer toward making skiing part of an afterthought, but I don't believe in that. Skiing is still the reason we come. Though you have to supplement the ski experience by nice amenities, the amenities are just frosting on the cake."

Courtesy of Alpine Meadows

A skier attacks an Alpine Meadows run called Peter's Peril. Lake Tahoe is visible in the background.

t was a summer day in 1977. Bill Killebrew was supposed to fly from South Lake Tahoe to San Francisco with his father, Hugh Killebrew, owner of Heavenly Valley. When he arrived at the airport a few minutes late because of a dental appointment, it wasn't surprising to the young Killebrew that his father had not waited for him. Setting out in his car toward the Bay Area, traffic was slowed due to a plane crash. He learned that it was his father's plane that was destroyed in a midair collision, killing his father and three of the resort's managers.

At age twenty-three, Bill Killebrew assumed control of Heavenly Valley and learned that the resort was millions of dollars in debt, basically bankrupt and on the brink of default. "It was after two drought years and, like all the resorts, we'd been hard hit. We had nothing in the bank. But I knew if I sold out I'd be getting nothing for the place. I didn't have anything to lose, so I tied a knot in the end of the rope and held on."

Amazingly, the young ski resort owner was prepared. He had had a unique relationship with his father. "My father always treated me like an adult, even when I was a small child. He allowed me to go to business meetings when I was very young. He taught me to listen first, analyze what was being said, and develop a course of action."

Hugh Killebrew had instilled a strong work ethic in his son whom he put on skis at age four. At twelve, Bill began to spend his summer vacations at the ski area. "My first job was policing the ground and picking up trash around the Pioneer Hut. By age fourteen I was working on lifts, digging a lot of holes, mostly." During his teens he learned about administration, first in the marketing department, then in the front office studying the approval process for building a ski lift. He also raced, well enough to be on the U.S. Ski Team's development team. By the time he was an undergraduate in business at University of California, Berkeley, Bill Killebrew was a partner in the resort.

On that fateful day when young Killebrew unexpectedly became the new leader, he gathered the staff at the resort. He remembers his first meeting of senior managers. "I told them that I couldn't make it without their help. I told them of our tough financial situation. I asked them to work with me. With their support we had a chance of success."

The first thing he did was to take what money he could find to upgrade a small snowmaking system already in place at Heavenly. He then reorganized the marketing department, insisting that Heavenly pursue foreign markets such as Japan, Mexico and Canada. He worked to reshape the mountain, widening ski slopes, changing runs into better fall-line terrain and allocating time to grooming and summer trail maintenance. "I tried to focus on skiing. People come to ski, not to sit in the lodges. I wanted better ski runs. Skiers like long runs on interesting terrain, and we wanted the average skier to have a good time."

All the planning and construction could not overcome unseasonably warm weather, however. "After my father's death, I'd gone ahead and spent a lot of money to put in the

B I L L

K I L L E B R E W

—

H E A V E N L Y

"Those were exciting years. We sometimes struggled and had our fair share of trouble, but I couldn't imagine doing anything else. To make a business grow, to work with great people, to live at an absolute pinnacle of excitement—I love it, but it also burned me out. The effort took much of my youth."

© *Carolyn Caddes*

"I've learned, through the values my father taught me, that a ski area builder is an entrepreneur, an individual following the convictions of a dream."

snowmaking, but by Thanksgiving there had been no snowfall. The snow we'd made had melted with warm temperatures." Killebrew was able to meet payroll, but he had laid off most of Heavenly's staff. Broke, his own bank account depleted and his credit cards maxed to their limit, Killebrew made an appointment to file bankruptcy papers the following week.

"I drove down to San Francisco to visit my girlfriend Abby. I was so broke I even had to borrow twenty dollars from her to drive back up to the lake." The weather forecast called for precipitation, but by the time Killebrew arrived at his stepmother's house, skies were clear.

"I went up to my father's study. I wanted him so much to be alive, but I had things to do." Sitting in his father's old leather chair he turned on the deck light and stared into the darkness. It was then he saw the first snowflake float down. "I was afraid to move, as if I did, it would stop. I kept watching the snow come down. I never went back to bed. I just sat there. By morning there was at least a foot of snow on the deck."

He drove to Heavenly's parking lot at 7:30 in the morning and found 300 employees waiting for orders. "Nobody had called them. They just came." Killebrew sent his secretary out for a case of champagne. "I took the bankruptcy papers, put them in the Governor's Cup Trophy and lit them on fire. Failure was no longer an option."

Heavenly opened its doors the day before Thanksgiving. Making a gutsy marketing decision, Killebrew advertised free skiing for two days. "Seven thousand people showed up on Wednesday, 9,000 on Thanksgiving. Though the skiing was free, we sold out of rentals, lessons and food. We were back in business."

For the next ten years Heavenly dominated the Sierra ski industry, recording huge ticket sales, creating worldwide attention through celebrity events and World Cup races. Between 1977 and 1985 skier days at the resort tripled in volume. No other major ski resort in Northern California matched its growth. Killebrew committed the resort to top-to-bottom snowmaking on both sides of the mountain. He invested $22 million on a system with 650 snow guns. "Every one of my managers thought I was wrong. They thought it a terrible waste of money. Sometimes you find yourself alone, but I knew it was the only way to go. Heavenly never lost money after 1987."

Feeling the strain of one-man rule, and not spending enough time with his family, Killebrew announced the sale of Heavenly to Kamori Kanko Company of Japan in November 1990.

"It wasn't so much financial as emotional. Heavenly is where I grew up and it had been a part of my family for thirty years. However, I thought the California ski industry had reached a point of diminishing returns. I was frustrated being a fireman and putting out fires, spending more time with taxes and lawyers as opposed to being an architect and builder. Skiing was getting away from old values I had known as a child."

After he sold Heavenly, Killebrew invested in an airplane leasing and sales business, allowing him to indulge in his passion for flying.

Unable to resist his first love, skiing, Killebrew became a partner in 1995 in Eldora Mountain Resort (formerly Lake Eldora), a small ski area outside Boulder, Colorado. Killebrew says, "It's a fun place, small and intimate, a short distance from Boulder, where kids can hop on a bus and come up for the day to snowboard and ski. It's more a love than a business for me. That's why I bought Eldora. It's a return to a love for the mountains and the fundamentals of the sport."

*Skiers at Heavenly
with Lake Tahoe
in the background.*

BILL JENSEN

—

A NEW

VISION

"I wanted to run a ski resort. I set a goal. By age forty, I wanted to be the general manager of a major ski area. That became my dream." When Bill Jensen was a lift supervisor at Mammoth Mountain in 1975, he already saw his future clearly.

ome might have scoffed at Jensen's plan to run a ski resort. The liberal arts graduate from Pepperdine had only moved to the mountains to take time out after college before deciding on a career. Working in lift operations, the twenty-three-year-old Californian earned $2.50 an hour. He'd only picked up skiing a few years before and was still learning.

"It didn't matter. The job was fun. But more than that, I really liked the ski business." Jensen achieved his dream when he was hired as general manager of Northstar-at-Tahoe at age thirty-nine.

"I'm not necessarily passionate about skiing like a Dave McCoy. He and others of his generation got into this business because they were passionate about the mountains, about the sport. Their generation had a different focus. I'm passionate about the business. I describe myself as a business person working in an industry I feel very strong about."

Jensen's apprenticeship included five years of ski operations and summer construction at Mammoth Mountain. He logged two seasons at Sun Valley as a lift supervisor. By age twenty-seven he had become the operations director for the construction of a new resort in Washington State, a job that exposed him to all facets of the ski industry including finance.

"In the 70s, the mind-set was 'if you build it they will come.' There were always lots of projects going on as ski resorts expanded themselves. I learned how to build lifts and trails. I dealt with everything from maintenance to sewage. I was very operations-focused. It was a period of what I consider an achievement phase, of learning about the running of a ski resort. However, these wouldn't be the skills needed to be successful in the 90s." Those skills came when he accepted a sales management position in the early 1980s with Kassbohrer All-Terrain Vehicles, Inc., one of the largest snow grooming vehicle companies in the world.

"I began learning the business side of the ski industry. I also began learning marketing aspects. The ski industry had shifted from 'if you build it they will come' to the idea that you had to convince them they should come."

From 1983 to 1988 Jensen rose to the position of vice president of Kassbohrer's track vehicle division for North America. Traveling extensively, visiting ski resorts throughout the country, Jensen built many relationships with ski resort personnel and owners. One was with Les Otten, the maverick owner of Sunday River, Maine. Considered by many industry insiders as a Bill Gates of skiing, Otten had helped revolutionize the ski industry by way of dynamic marketing strategies and fast-paced change during the 1980s. He'd turned his once small, isolated ski area into a seven-resort group that dominated the northeastern ski industry.

"Though I was successful and enjoyed work in sales, I'd never lost sight of my dream of running a ski resort. When Les asked me to come work for him at Sunday River, I thought it was the appropriate opportunity to get back towards my goal."

© Carolyn Caddes

"I think you have to have a passion for what you do. I studied Dave McCoy. He cared about his people; he cared about the guest.
He was really focused on providing a great experience.
I was naive enough to look at Dave and think I could one day have as much impact."

With Jensen as vice president of marketing, Sunday River became known for its innovative and creative schemes such as comparison marketing. Seemingly, Sunday River did things quicker than its competitors. Jensen learned the dynamics between beds and ticket sales. "Les used to say, 'Heads on beds mean butts in seats.'" Sunday River marketed its snowmaking system more than others. The resort created a reputation for always having the best snow. "We called it 'retail snow.'" Not afraid to try anything new or break the rules of traditional competition, Jensen utilized Sunday River's marketing muscle to woo increasing crowds. In the three seasons he worked at the ski resort, Sunday River grew from 250,000 to 460,000 skier visits annually.

Jensen brought his strategies to the Sierra Nevada when he was hired by Fibreboard Corporation to run Northstar-at-Tahoe in 1991. Utilizing the key ingredients that had made Sunday River successful, Jensen helped Northstar increase its annual ticket sales from 250,000 to 500,000 within five years. He developed an electronic frequent-skier program called "Vertical Plus" that rewards skiers for vertical feet skied with discounts on tickets and premiums, the first of its kind in the country. Under his management, Fibreboard's Resort Group division grew to include Sierra Ski Ranch, renamed Sierra-at-Tahoe, and Bear Mountain Ski Resort in Southern California, to become the largest ski resort operator in California.

"Although we operated several resorts, I still believe that each ski area needs its own personality and own style. That's why it's important to keep the corporate side in the background and create an environment to allow the employees who are driven by the skiing lifestyle to make day-to-day decisions. The employees are the ones who need to be given the right and the responsibility to satisfy the customer."

Booth Creek Partners purchased Fibreboard's Resort Group division in October 1996 and elevated Jensen to chief executive officer overseeing the operation of ten ski areas nationwide, including the three in California. His management skills determined the ski experience for close to two million annual skier visits.

In an age of consolidation and financial squeeze, his senses are constantly acute to the rapid changes in a transformed ski industry. "The reality is, I enjoy this business. When I was twenty-three I hoped to make a contribution to the ski industry. As I've matured I realize just having the opportunity to make a difference is what it is about. I laugh when I overhear that ski area jobs aren't real jobs. These are real jobs. This is a real business, and I feel really fortunate and lucky to be a part of it."

"In the past, ski resorts looked at marketing as a necessary evil, one of the last priorities to be dealt with. But the industry changed from a sport in the 70s, to a recreation activity in the 80s, to an entertainment business in the 90s. Les saw the need for marketing to be the driving force behind the business. You have to make the point that you have a different product than anybody else."

THE

FUTURE

OF THE

SKI

INDUSTRY

—

BY

STU

CAMPBELL

In the fall of 1978 I came into the high Sierra, having accepted a management job at a major Lake Tahoe ski resort. Raised in Vermont—always in or at least on the periphery of—the Eastern ski industry, I came with an enthusiasm dampened by skepticism. I didn't know what I might find.

A pall-like, incessant overcast had fallen over skiing in the Eastern U.S. In the days before powerful snowmaking systems and groomers that bring slopes back to life overnight, rain, recession, thaw, bitter cold, pessimism and gasoline shortages plagued ski areas in the Northeast. Skiing seemed a sport, a business, a way of life in decline. Prospects for growth seemed remote, and innovative concepts were met with a "you-can't-*do*-that" response.

Like so many of the mountain dreamers on these pages, I was enchanted by the amber afternoon light that cast long shadows across apparently endless, skiable Sierra bowls, hypnotized by the myriad snow conditions beneath widespread trees, where light slanted as if into a cathedral. I never dreamed so much snow could fall in so short a time.

But what inspired me most was the open receptiveness of people like Nic Fiore, Bill Killebrew, Vern Sprock, Maury Rasmussen, Stan Tomlinson, Werner Schuster, Dave McCoy, the Mammoth Mountain Race Department and dozens of others who retained a fresh western optimism.

Unguarded, visionary and individualistic as all hell, each exuded a "that's-a-good-idea-let's-*do*-that" spirit. I quickly came to respect them as smart, tough men, men who adopted then adapted to a spectacular and harsh environment, men who opened the Sierra backcountry then invited the rest of us to play in it.

Skiing, we mourn, has become more of an industry in the 80s and 90s, less a risky, pioneering lifestyle. As the realities of weather, seasonality, escalating operating costs, debt, environmentalist obstruction, risk management and litigation sink in, operators like Killebrew, Nick Badami and Bill Jensen blended business acumen with their considerable backgrounds in the sport.

But even they are being replaced by slick marketeers and cautious CPA-CEOs committed to a preconceived bottom line.

The result, of course, is a more convenient, user-friendly environment: snow guarantees and near-perfect riding surfaces. The experience is homogenized, almost sterilized, as guests are insulated from the cold and glare, protected from risk and as some would insist, isolated from their own spirits.

The mom-and-pop operations have all but disappeared in the Sierra, as they have everywhere else. Skiing is now corporatized and consolidated, financed by large international resort interests. Sierra ski areas no longer cater only to locals, Californians and Nevadans. They come from the East, from Europe, the Orient and Latin America. They come from the inner cities and from cultures that seem alien to mountains.

Many come with one board instead of two, with differing attitudes about clothing and food, music, people who have preceded them and services they expect. They seem *so* different one wonders if in fact "ski" resorts should be managed by the middle-aged white males that do so now.

At first we look askance at this new generation of snow-sliding men and women. A closer look—eye contact—reveals the same joy, the same undaunted determination we have seen reflected in the eyes of Alex Cushing, Charlie Proctor, Luggi Foeger, Jimmie Huega and Tamara McKinney. Among them, I wager, are multiple reincarnations of Bill Berry and Dave McCoy.

So the Sierra spirit is alive and in good hands. The valley floors may fill with condos and commerce. The lower pistes may always be covered with groomed, machine-made snow that is boringly predictable. But as Jo Marillac pitched to the International Olympic Committee before the 1960 Winter Olympic Games at Squaw Valley, man can build almost anything, but he can't build mountains. Ours will always be there, frosted by real snow.

Look to the peaks, and dream on.

Stowe, Vermont, February 1997

Stu Campbell was once
vice president of Skier Services
at Heavenly Resort.
He has been
Instructional Editor for
SKI magazine since the
mid-70s, and is a
longtime examiner for the
Professional Ski Instructors
of America.
He has authored two books
on ski techniques,
Ski With the Big Boys *and*
The Way to Ski, *and*
twelve other titles on a variety
of nonfiction subjects.

© Tom Lippert

INDEX

The Ansel Adams photograph on page 25 is ©1997 by the Trustees of the Ansel Adams Publishing Rights Trust. All rights reserved.

The photographs by Ray Atkeson are reprinted with permission of Rick Schafer Photography of Portland, Oregon. Photographs by Ray Atkeson on pages 109 and 121 are from the American Landscapes collection.

I wish to thank the following for the use of photographs from their collections: Alpine Meadows, Auburn Ski Club, William B. Berry, Craig Beck, Jill Kinmont Boothe, Peggy Dean, Dodge Ridge, Nic Fiore, Robert Frohlich, Babette Haueisen, Kirkwood Ski Resort, Bill Klein, Bud Klein, Tom Lippert, Mammoth Mountain, Jo Marillac, National Park Service, Yosemite, Northstar-at-Tahoe, Sandy Poulsen, Ralph Purdy, Vern and Bobbie Sprock, Squaw Valley Ski Corporation, Sugar Bowl Resort, the Rasmussen family and Carson White.